WILD FOOD, GARDEN FOOD
GATHER AND COOK
THROUGH THE YEAR

By

CHARLOTTE POPESCU

CAVALIER PAPERBACKS

Published by Cavalier Paperbacks 2008

Cavalier Paperbacks
Burnham House,
Upavon,
Wilts SN9 6DU

www.cavalierpaperbacks.co.uk

ISBN 978-1-899470-28-0

Printed and bound in Great Britain by Cromwell Press,
White Horse Industrial Park, Trowbridge

CONTENTS

INTRODUCTION

In this book I cover vegetables, cultivated fruit, edible garden flowers and wild food (greens, flowers, mushrooms and fruits) as they become available through the year, featuring each one in the month when it is at its best. I am not going to include every single plant that it is possible to grow or that you can gather in the wild; I am going to concentrate on a balanced selection of vegetables, wild greens, fruits, mushrooms and edible flowers that you can grow or search for in the countryside and use in the kitchen month by month. These will be plants that from personal experience seem to be the most practical to cook and eat – plants that will keep you almost self sufficient in fruits, vegetables, greens and mushrooms – plants that are relatively easy to grow and that do not take up too much space.

Realistically you're probably not going to have the time to find all the wild plants and fungi mentioned but you may be interested in how many edible plants there are. On the subject of the mushrooms mentioned in this book, this is not intended to be a guide to identification of edible mushrooms. You need to buy a good, illustrated guide or find a mushroom expert so that you can be sure you have identified edible mushrooms before you eat them. What is for sure is that there is a lot of free food out there and you will be amazed by how many weeds you can actually eat.

I won't include asparagus, sweet corn (maize is a large plant that only produces 2 or 3 cobs), the more exotic vegetables such as peppers, chillis and aubergines for which in these unpredictable summers a greenhouse is preferable. I won't include cauliflowers that take up a lot of space and can be disappointing or globe artichokes. I will include the wild greens and edible flowers that are the most worthwhile to pick and eat or use to make wine. Produce will be included in the month or months when it is likely to be at its optimum.

QUICK GUIDE

MID WINTER – January and February

SOW VEGETABLES: Broad beans, onions, early lettuces, garlic; force rhubarb.

PICK FROM THE VEGETABLE PATCH: Kale, endives, winter and savoy cabbages; force chicory for chicons and continue to dig Jerusalem artichokes.

GATHER FROM THE WILD: Lesser celandine, bitter vetch, corn salad, hairy bittercress, young dandelion leaves, young Alexanders leaves.

GATHER MUSHROOMS: Scarlet elf cups, Jew's ears and velvet shanks.

EARLY SPRING – March and April

SOW VEGETABLES: Broad beans, potatoes, onions, beetroot, radishes, parsnips, spinach, mangetout and peas, carrots, salad leaves and Swiss chard, cabbages, dwarf French beans, rocket, runner beans, spring onions. Plant out seedlings such as Brussels sprouts, calabrese and sprouting broccoli.

PICK FROM THE VEGETABLE PATCH: Over-wintering lettuce, purple sprouting broccoli, early broad beans, forced rhubarb.

GATHER FROM THE WILD: Flowers such as coltsfoot, primroses, cowslips, gorse and broom; Ramsons (wild garlic), garlic mustard, dandelion, young nettles, Alexanders stems and leaves, hop shoots, lungwort, golden saxifrage, beech leaves, sheep and wood sorrel, ground elder and fat hen. In the wild herbs category you can pick cow parsley, comfrey, herb bennet, wild chives and lemon balm.

GATHER MUSHROOMS: St George's mushrooms, morels.

GATHER FROM THE SEA SHORE: Sea beet.

LATE SPRING - May

SOW VEGETABLES: Broccoli, and Brussels sprout seedlings, French and runner beans. Plant out courgette and tomato plants, squash and pumpkins, outdoor cucumbers, leeks and turnips.
PICK FROM THE VEGETABLE PATCH: Salad leaves/lettuces, rocket, spinach, radishes, spring onions, early potatoes.
GATHER GARDEN FRUIT: Gooseberries.
GATHER FROM THE WILD: Hawthorn leaves and flowers, goat's beard, woodruff, red valerian, nipplewort, hawkbit, scurvy grass, wild fennel, brooklime, ground ivy, tansy, lime leaves and flowers. Continue to pick Alexanders and chickweed.
GATHER MUSHROOMS: Fairy ring mushrooms.
ON THE SEA SHORE: Rock samphire.

EARLY SUMMER - June

SOW VEGETABLES: Beetroot, carrots, French beans, salad leaves and rocket, radishes, spring onions, turnips.
PICK FROM THE VEGETABLE PATCH: Peas, sugar snap peas and mangetout, broad beans, salad leaves, radishes, spinach, good King Henry; dig new potatoes.
GATHER GARDEN FLOWERS: Nasturtiums.
GATHER FROM THE WILD: Elderflowers, daisies, clover, bistort, pignuts, sweet cicely, corn and common sow thistle, milk thistle, lesser burdock, mallow, cow parsley.
GATHER MUSHROOMS: Fairy ring mushrooms, ceps.
GATHER FROM THE SEA SHORE: Dulse, sea beet, marsh and rock samphire.

MID TO LATE SUMMER - July and August

SOW VEGETABLES Plant final crops of beetroot, kale, radicchio and endive, mizuna, chinese mustard leaves, pak choi, carrots, radishes, spinach.
PICK FROM THE VEGETABLE PATCH: Lettuce, French and

8

runner beans. Continue to pick beetroot, mangetout, asparagus peas, radishes, rocket, spinach and dig up carrots and potatoes.

GATHER GARDEN FLOWERS: Lavender, nasturtiums, marigold and rose petals; also lemon geranium leaves.

GATHER GARDEN FRUIT: Strawberries, raspberries, redcurrants, blackcurrants, blueberries, cherries, mulberries, plums.

GATHER FROM THE WILD: Blackberries, crab apples; also still available: lime flowers, hogweed, wild marjoram, meadowsweet, lady's bedstraw, rest-harrow, white horehound.

GATHER MUSHROOMS: Parasols, chanterelles, giant and common puffballs, hedgehog fungus.

GATHER FROM THE SEA SHORE: Sea beet, rock samphire, sea purslane.

EARLY AUTUMN – September

SOW VEGETABLES: Over-wintering lettuces, Chinese mustard leaves, turnips.

PICK FROM THE VEGETABLE PATCH: Beetroot, carrots, chard, courgettes, cucumbers, lettuces, rocket, runner and French beans, tomatoes, pumpkins, squashes.

GATHER FROM THE GARDEN: Nasturtium leaves.

GATHER GARDEN FRUIT: Apples, pears, raspberries, damsons, figs.

GATHER FROM THE WILD: You can still pick blackberries and crab apples and you should now also find bilberries, elderberries, hazelnuts, wild damsons and sloes (sometimes ready at this time). For wild greens you can gather nettles which if cut back earlier in the year will be growing up again, good King Henry, chickweed, horseradish, chicory and dandelion roots, poppy seeds.

GATHER MUSHROOMS: Field and horse mushrooms, shaggy ink caps as well as chanterelles and ceps.

GATHER FROM THE SEA SHORE: Sea beet, samphire.

MID AUTUMN - October

SOW VEGETABLES: Garlic, broad beans, rhubarb.

PICK FROM THE VEGETABLE PATCH: winter spinach, Swiss chard, kale, radicchio and endive.

GATHER GARDEN FRUIT: Apples, quinces.

GATHER FROM THE WILD: Rosehips, haws, walnuts, sweet chestnuts, sloes and bullaces.

GATHER MUSHROOMS: Parasols, saffron milk caps, horn of plenty, oyster mushrooms.

GATHER FROM THE SEA SHORE: Sea beet.

LATE AUTUMN - November

PICK FROM YOUR VEGETABLE PATCH: Parsnips, swede, celeriac, Jerusalem artichokes, kale, salsify and scorzonera.

GATHER GARDEN FRUIT: Medlars.

GATHER FROM THE WILD: Alexanders, chickweed, silverweed and its roots, cat's tail, star of Bethlehem, white waterlily, evening primrose.

GATHER WILD MUSHROOMS: Honey fungus, wood and field blewits, saffron milk caps, oyster mushrooms.

EARLY WINTER - December

PICK FROM YOUR VEGETABLE PATCH: Leeks, radicchio, endive, Brussels sprouts and continue to pick Jerusalem artichokes and kale. Also salad herbs such as winter purslane and salad burnet.

GATHER FROM THE WILD: Continue to gather haws and pick Alexanders, chickweed, yarrow, goosegrass, common wintercress, shepherd's purse.

GATHER MUSHROOMS: Jew's ears, velvet shanks.

GATHER FROM THE SEA SHORE: Sea beet.

MID WINTER
January and February

It's a new year but you *can* have vegetables to harvest at this time of year and there *are* wild greens worth picking in the countryside. It's probably best to wait until February but then you can sow broad beans, garlic and early lettuces under glass. You can also force rhubarb.

In your vegetable garden you will still be able to dig up Jerusalem artichokes, a prolific free food – artichokes will re-appear every year with no effort or cost to you! February is also the time to plant new Jerusalem artichoke tubers – beg some tubers off a friend or buy some from a good garden centre – you will have artichokes for years to come. You should still have some leeks, Brussels sprouts and the wonderful Nero di Toscana (also known as Cavolo Nero or Black or Russian Kale). Ready for harvest now will be your winter and savoy cabbages. You may also have some carrots, swedes or parsnips still to dig up. You can also grow chicory and force or blanch it for chicons in January and February. Endives can be harvested along with salsify.

For fruit, you may have some apples that you stored in October or November. This is obviously a sparse time of year for fruits from the garden but in the fields and down country lanes you should be able to find various greens that you can use in the kitchen and possibly some fungi. You should find lesser celandine, bitter vetch, corn salad (lamb's lettuce) and hairy bittercress, young dandelion leaves and on the fungi front you may come across scarlet elf cups, Jew's ears and velvet shanks which are all edible.

CULTIVATED VEGETABLES

WINTER AND SAVOY CABBAGE - Brassica oleracea

Cabbage along with kale, cauliflower, broccoli, kohlrabi and Brussels sprouts all belong to the same species of plant: Brassica oleracea, commonly known as Brassicas, which are all descended from the wild cabbage. Cabbage has a long history, going back 4,000 years. Between China and Mongolia horsemen learned to preserve this vegetable in brine and it became the staple diet for the builders of the Great Wall of China. It was a popular vegetable in Greek and Roman times both as a food and for medicinal purposes. Greek mythology tells us that the cabbage actually sprang from the fallen tears of a Thracian king, Lycurgus, who was killed by Dionysus for uprooting some of his favourite grapevines. The Celts may well have introduced cabbage to Britain in the 4th century BC. The cultivation of cabbage spread across northern Europe into Germany, Poland and Russia and became very popular. Seeds sown in May and transplanted in June will provide savoy cabbages from January to March. Likewise for winter cabbages in January and February transplant seedlings in July.

BRAISED SAVOY CABBAGE
Serves 4

1 savoy cabbage, shredded
175g, 6oz unsmoked streaky bacon, chopped
1 onion, peeled and sliced
a little olive oil
salt, pepper and pinch of paprika

Cook the cabbage for 5 minutes in boiling, salted water and drain. Fry the bacon in its own fat until crisp, then add the onion and cook until soft. Add the cabbage, adding a little olive oil if necessary and season with salt, pepper and a little paprika. This would go well with pork or eggs.

KALE - **Brassica oleracea**

Kale has long been cultivated in northern Europe but the Scots are perhaps the keenest kale eaters and their kale brose (a kale and oatmeal soup) used to form part of their staple diet. Kale is extremely hardy and can withstand very low temperatures and therefore is not killed off by frosts. It is a really useful vegetable to grow for winter use as the fresh young leaves can be used in salads. Hungry Gap is a rape kale, usually harvested from February onwards. It can be planted from March under cloches if you want to use the baby leaves in salads and they will be ready 8 – 12 weeks from sowing. Red Russian Kale is good for this. Otherwise plant seeds outside from April to June and you should be able to harvest your kale from December but it is especially useful in January and February when greens are scarce. Nero di Toscana produces an excellent crop - I grow this one every year. Redbor is a red variety for picking through the winter and young leaves can also be used in salads. I have tried Pentland Brig which lasts well through the winter, producing curly edged leaves. It is very useful – not only can leaves be picked right through January and February but later on spears appear that can be used like sprouting broccoli. Kale is rich in iron, Vitamin C and calcium. Only pick the young leaves as older leaves can be bitter. If picked regularly you should get a good supply over a number of weeks.

ORIENTAL-STYLE STIR FRIED KALE
Serves 4

1 tbsp sesame oil
1 small piece root ginger, peeled
2 cloves of garlic, peeled and chopped
450g, 1lb curly kale
1 onion, peeled and thinly sliced
3 tbsp soya sauce
3 tbsp sherry
1 tbsp sesame seeds

Heat the sesame oil in a wok and add the ginger and garlic. After 30 seconds add the kale and onion. Stir fry for a couple of minutes and then add the soya sauce and sherry. Bring to the boil and serve immediately sprinkled with sesame seeds.

KALE AND CARROT AU GRATIN
Serves 4 – 6

300ml, ½pt Marigold Swiss vegetable bouillon stock
1 onion, peeled and chopped
75g, 3oz long grain rice
1 tsp fresh thyme, chopped
2 large carrots, peeled and sliced
1kg, 2.2lb curly kale
100g, 4oz ricotta
75g, 3oz mature Cheddar cheese, grated
pinch of nutmeg + salt and pepper
2 tbsp wholemeal breadcrumbs

Pour the stock into a saucepan and add the onion and thyme and bring to the boil. Add the rice and simmer until the rice is cooked. This should take about 15 minutes. Add the sliced carrots about 5 minutes before the end of the cooking time. Steam the kale for no more than 3 or 4 minutes. Transfer the rice to an ovenproof dish and mix in the kale, ricotta and half the cheese. Sprinkle the breadcrumbs and rest of the cheese on the top and dribble with olive oil. Cook in the oven at gas mark 4, 180°C (350°F) for about 20 minutes and then finish browning the top under the grill.

CHICORY Grown for Chicons - Chichorium intybus

Sow chicory seeds in May or June. In November when the leaves have died down, cut them off about 2.5cm, 1in above the roots and lift them carefully. Trim the roots, cutting off any side-shoots. To force and blanch, plant four or five roots in a pot of soil and after watering cover with another pot to exclude light. Keep reasonably warm and chicons (conical heads of crisp, white slightly bitter leaves) will be about 15cm, 6in tall and ready to harvest six weeks later. You can cut these off at the base and leave the roots which will grow a second crop of chicons. Varieties to try are Sugar Loaf whose leaves can be picked in the summer or Witloof. You can boil, steam or braise chicons or use in salads. Bitterness can be reduced by blanching the vegetable for two minutes in boiling water. Chicory contains the nutrient inulin which is known to promote good bacteria and helps detox the colon.

CHICONS WITH LEMON SAUCE
Serves 4

4 chicons, outer leaves, root base and inner core removed
juice of 1 lemon
300ml, ½pt white béchamel sauce
2 egg yolks
25g, 1oz butter
2 tbsp breadcrumbs

Cut the chicons in half lengthways and put in a pan of salted, boiling water. Boil for 10 minutes, then drain. Add lemon juice to the white sauce and stir in the egg yolks. Gently heat the sauce. Put the chicons in a buttered ovenproof dish, pour the sauce over, sprinkle with breadcrumbs and dot with butter. Bake in the oven at gas mark 4, 180°C (350°F) for about 10 minutes.

IN THE WILD
Wild Greens

LESSER CELANDINE - Ranunculus ficaria

One of the first green plants to appear in January along with snowdrops, lesser celandine grows on roadside verges, in hedgerows, damp woods and bare patches of ground throughout Britain. It is a hairless perennial and has green shiny heart-shaped leaves with a mottled appearance. Bright yellow flowers come out not long after the leaves so it is easy to distinguish. Both the leaves and roots have been used for medicinal purposes in the past, especially to treat haemorrhoids. Leaves can be used in salads and sandwiches or if you pick enough leaves and stalks you can cook them like spinach. Lesser celandine was William Wordsworth's favourite plant and its flowers have been carved on his tomb. He wrote a poem, The Lesser Celandine 'There is a Flower, the Lesser Celandine, That shrinks, like many more, from cold and rain; And, the first moment that the sun may shine, Bright as the sun himself, 'tis out again! ...'

BITTER VETCH Also known as Heath Pea
Lathyrus montanus

Bitter vetch is an edible tuber from the pea family. The roots are worth eating. However you will probably only be able to identify the plant when it's in flower between April and July. Flowers are sweet pea-type red purple; after flowering, seed pods appear. The leaves are greeny-blue. Mark the spot where you've seen the plants in flower and go back in the winter to dig up the roots. It is found most prevalently in the North and West on moors, ungrazed heathland and woods. The roots which are about 10cm, 4in below the surface should be peeled and chopped and cooked as other root vegetables. They taste like liquorice and have a bitter taste but they have one distinctive benefit – they can stave off hunger pangs so if you're on a diet they could be useful! In Medieval times bitter vetch was used as a hunger suppressant in times when the crops failed. King Charles II gave it to those mistresses that he believed were too fat. Monks used the plant to treat patients at the Soutra Aisle monastery near Edinburgh. Apparently in the Western Isles of Scotland bitter vetch roots are eaten fresh and raw.

CORN SALAD Also known as Lamb's lettuce
Valerianella locusta

Corn salad grows all over Britain in the wild. The leaves should be gathered in the early spring and used in salad. You can also pick the leaves in the autumn. Cultivated corn salad is usually called lamb's lettuce and is available as seed from catalogues and you can plant some in your veg patch. The leaves go well with beetroot but to coincide with beetroot in your garden you need to pick the leaves in July and August. In March and April use corn salad to make an interesting mixed salad.

**WILD CORN SALAD
WITH EGG AND RED PEPPER
Serves 2 – 3**

*Handful of corn salad + some other lettuce leaves
1 red pepper, sliced
1 avocado, peeled, stoned and sliced
3 hard boiled eggs, peeled and halved
4 tbsp walnut oil + 2 tbsp wine vinegar
salt and pepper
50g, 2oz croutons*

Arrange the corn salad, lettuce leaves, red pepper, avocado and eggs on a plate or in a bowl. Mix together the walnut oil, vinegar, salt and pepper and dress the salad. Scatter the croutons over the top. Serve immediately.

HAIRY BITTERCRESS - Cardamine hirsute

This is common on rocks and dunes, in gardens on the bare soil of flower beds, ploughed fields or wasteland. Hairy bittercress is an annual herb and one of the first worthwhile plants to be found at the beginning of the year. The leaves can be eaten through the winter. They taste quite bitter and mustardy so should be mixed with some blander greens. The plant flowers from March to September.

Mushrooms

JEW'S EAR
Hirneola auricular-Judae

This is an edible jelly like fungus that can be found any time of the year growing usually on dead elder and sometimes on beech trees. Jew's ears are pale brown in colour and really do resemble human ears in size, shape and texture. As the fungus gets older it goes black and hard. It is one of the few fungi which has the ability to withstand freezing temperatures. This is a useful attribute, since it develops new growths in January, which is normally the coldest month of the year. It can actually freeze solid, and when thawed out, shows no ill effects. The name comes from the story that Judas Iscariot hung himself from an elder tree after betraying Christ, and the elder became known as 'Judas Tree'. So elders are weak and hollow-hearted and soon decay and the ears of Judas soon materialise. Judas's ear gradually changed to Jew's ear – these mushrooms are also known as monkey's ears. They need to be cooked or stewed in a little stock until they become tender. Don't fry them – I tried this and they kept popping, like popcorn, and flew out of the frying pan on to the floor.

SCARLET ELF CUPS - Sarcoscypha coccinea

These scarlet-coloured mushrooms appear in January and February. They are cup-shaped with the margins becoming tatty as the mushroom gets bigger. Scarlet elf-cups can be found on dead wood or twigs often growing in a cluster especially in the West. They are edible.

EARLY SPRING
March and April

March and April are prime months for sowing your vegetables. You should plant any of the following during this period: broad beans, potatoes, onions, beetroot, radishes, parsnips, spinach, mangetout and peas, carrots, salad leaves and Swiss chard. Plant out seedlings such as Brussels sprouts, calabrese and sprouting broccoli.

If you have only room for a few vegetables then I would recommend growing some beetroot, spinach, mangetout and salad leaves. When it comes to gathering food from your garden you will probably not have that much available at this time of the year. This is traditionally known as 'The Hungry Gap'. Purple sprouting broccoli is an ideal vegetable to make space for in your vegetable patch or allotment – delicious, easy to grow and ready for picking now. Spring cabbage also comes into its own now but can be difficult to grow. You might also have some over-wintering lettuce or some winter spinach. If you plant some mixed salad leaves under a cloche in February such as rocket and various Chinese leaves such as Red Giant Mustard and Mizuna these should be ready for picking now. Rhubarb is also in season.

Take a walk in the countryside and gather some interesting edible flowers and weeds. You can pick coltsfoot, primroses, cowslips, gorse and broom flowers. For greens you should be able to find wild garlic, garlic mustard, dandelions, young nettles, Alexanders, hop shoots, fat hen and good King Henry, ground elder, golden saxifrage, lungwort, lady's smock, sorrel and beech leaves. Plaintain and charlock are two troublesome weeds that you can actually eat. On the wild herbs front you can pick cow parsley, hogweed, comfrey, herb bennet and lemon balm. You may be able to find St George's mushrooms which are traditionally around on 23rd April and morels now come into season. If you live near the sea or take a trip to the sea side, you should be able to find sea beet and sea kale.

CULTIVATED VEGETABLES

PURPLE SPROUTING BROCCOLI Brassica oleracea

Broccoli is an Italian word, derived from the Latin brachium, meaning branch or arm and indeed broccoli does look similar to the large branch of a tree. Broccoli certainly seems to have originated in Italy and was probably developed from the cabbage plant, possibly by the Etruscans who were around about 1100BC. The Romans conquered Etruria, today's Tuscany, in 200BC and Apicius the famous Roman cookery writer uses it in his recipes. We know that broccoli spread from Italy and France to Northern Europe and arrived in Britain in the 18th century. At that time it seemed to be known as Italian Asparagus.

Purple sprouting broccoli is a popular variety to grow in this country because it is hardy and produces a succession of small flowerheads for cropping over a long season from winter and especially valuable in spring when not many other vegetables are in season. You can either grow it from seeds in a propagator or greenhouse or buy plants to plant out in May. They do take up a lot of space, grow quite tall and have a long growing season so be warned! Harvest the heads before they have a chance to flower. If you harvest regularly without stripping each plant completely, the side shoots will keep providing more heads so you should be able to keep picking for at least six weeks.

Broccoli is a highly nutritious vegetable containing vitamins A, and C and is an excellent source of calcium, and a good source for potassium and iron. It is also loaded with phytochemicals such as beta carotene, indoles and isothiocyanates and contains sulforaphane, a compound which has an antibiotic effect and may help against stomach ulcers and cancer. Calabrese is the name for summer sprouting broccoli – see page 132.

PASTA WITH BROCCOLI, TUNA AND ANCHOVIES
Serves 4

350g, 12oz pasta tubes
4 anchovy fillets and their oil
2 cloves of garlic, peeled and chopped
225g, 8oz purple sprouting broccoli
1 red pepper
1 tsp chilli flakes (optional)
185g, 7oz can of tuna in oil

Cook the pasta according to the packet instructions. To make the sauce, pour the anchovies and oil into a frying pan. Fry for a couple of minutes with the garlic and then stir in the broccoli, red pepper and chilli flakes if using. Cover and cook for a few minutes. Stir in the tuna with its oil. Pour over the drained pasta and serve immediately.

PURPLE SPROUTING BROCCOLI
WITH WALNUT BUTTER
Serves 3 – 4

450g, 1lb purple sprouting broccoli
50g, 2oz butter
25g, 1oz walnuts, crushed

Steam or boil the broccoli in a very little water for no more than 3 or 4 minutes. In the meantime melt the butter in a small saucepan and cook until it turns brown. Tip in the walnuts and allow to heat through for 30 seconds. Transfer the broccoli to a serving dish and pour the walnut butter over the top. Serve at once.

SPRING CABBAGE - Brassica oleracea

Spring greens or cabbage and also primo types have much looser leaves than other cabbages. These come into season from April to June. For spring cabbage, which can be either spring greens or hearted cabbage, sow in early August in a seedbed and plant out in the middle of September. Timing is all important – sow too early and the plants may grow too large to withstand a hard winter; too late and they won't have enough time to develop beyond the seedling stage before the winter sets in. From February, spring cabbages will mature quickly.

STIR FRIED CABBAGE WITH HORSERADISH
Serves 4

2 tbsp olive oil
1 spring cabbage
1 onion, peeled and sliced thinly
1 garlic clove, peeled and crushed
1 tbsp lemon juice
150ml, ¼pt Greek yoghurt
2 tsp creamed horseradish

Heat the oil in a wok. Shred the cabbage and stir fry in the wok with the onion and garlic. Keep turning the cabbage so that it doesn't burn. Mix the lemon juice, yoghurt and horseradish. Drain the cabbage, getting rid of as much excess oil as possible. Stir in the yoghurt mixture and serve.

CABBAGE STEAMED IN THE WOK
Serves 4 – 6

This is stir fried/steamed in the wok without oil so a very healthy and tasty way to serve cabbage.

1 spring cabbage, shredded
90ml, 3fl oz Marigold Swiss vegetable bouillon stock
1 tbsp sunflower seeds

Put the shredded cabbage in a wok and add the stock. Cover and steam for 5 – 8 minutes. Add the sunflower seeds, give it a good stir and serve.

RHUBARB - Rheum rhaponticum

Rhubarb originated in China around 2700BC but was not culivated in Europe until the 1700s. It is mostly served sweet and thought of as a fruit but is actually a vegetable. We grow rhubarb for the stalks; the leaves are poisonous. If you want to grow it, buy it as a crown with one or two fat buds on it. You need to plant the crowns in late autumn or winter. You should wait until the second year before harvesting between March and early June. An earlier harvest can be achieved by forcing - cover your rhubarb in January with a bucket or large flowerpot and eat rhubarb in February. To cook rhubarb, cut into chunks and stew with sugar or roast with honey dribbled over it. Use to fill pastries and pies or as a base for a fool. A tart sauce can be made to serve with oily fish such as mackerel. You can also make jam.

RHUBARB AMBER
Serves 4 – 6

Shortcrust pastry lining a greased 20cm, 8in flan tin
450g, 1lb rhubarb, washed and sliced

strip of lemon rind
75g, 3oz granulated sugar
2 egg yolks, beaten
2 tbsp melted butter

Meringue topping
2 egg whites
100g, 4oz caster sugar

Bake the pastry case blind in the oven at gas mark 4, 180°C (350°F), for 10 minutes. Cook the rhubarb with the strip of lemon, the sugar and a little water until soft. Beat to a purée. Stir in the egg yolks and butter. Spread over the pastry base. Bake in the oven at gas mark 4, 180°C (350°F) for 15 minutes. In the meantime beat the egg whites until stiff and then gradually beat in the caster sugar. Swirl over the rhubarb and return to the oven for 20 minutes until nicely browned on top.

RHUBARB AND GINGER JAM
Makes 5lb, 2.5kg

1.5kg, 3lb rhubarb, washed and cut into chunks
1.5kg, 3lb granulated sugar
120ml, 4fl oz lemon juice
25g, 1oz root ginger, bruised

Put the rhubarb in a bowl layered with the sugar. Add the lemon juice and leave overnight. Transfer to a large saucepan and add the ginger. Bring to the boil and boil until setting point is reached. Remove the ginger. Pour into jars and seal.

IN THE WILD
Wild Flowers

COLTSFOOT - **Tussilago farfara**

The flowers of coltsfoot come out at the end of February and so you can pick them through March. The leaves, strangely, only come out after the flowers have died, and can be picked from April until July. Coltsfoot grows all over Britain. Why this plant is named 'coltsfoot' is uncertain – there seems very little connection with a colt, possibly the leaves which are cottony with white hairs on the underside appear to be like that of a colt. It can be found by streams, on hillsides, on the edges of woodland and on roadside verges and waste places. This plant has an aggressive root system (like mint) so will spread freely. You can use the flowers, which have an aniseed flavour in salads or to make wine or you can put the petals in sponge cakes or in ice cream. The leaves are meant to be very effective in a drink for anyone suffering from a cough or asthma. All parts of coltsfoot contain a mucilage which is good for coughs and bronchitis – the Latin name 'Tussilago farfara' also indicates that the plant was considered good as a cough medicine because 'tussis' is cough in Latin.

You can use 25g, 1oz of leaves combined with 1 litre or 2 pints of water. Bring to the boil and then simmer until the liquid reduces by half. Sweeten the drink with honey and drink as much as you like. You can also use dried leaves or flowers to make tea. Alternatively boil chopped leaves and stems, extract the liquid and boil with sugar to make a syrup, similar to barley sugar. Dried leaves are also used in herbal tobaccos.

COLTSFOOT WINE

2 litres, 4pts coltsfoot flowers
juice and rind of 1 large orange and 1 lemon
1kg, 2.2lb granulated sugar
2 litres, 4pts water
15g, ½oz yeast

Pick the flowers and measure them by putting them in a 1 litre or 2 pint jug, without pressing them down too much. Transfer to a large bowl and add the juice and rind of the orange and lemon. Dissolve the sugar in the water over a low heat. Allow to cool and then pour over the flowers. Add the yeast and leave for 5 days. Pour into a glass jar or cask. Stand on a tray and keep in a warm room. After a while fermentation will start and froth will pour over the side of the container. When the frothing has stopped cork or insert an air lock. When fermentation is complete, ie. gas bubbles are no longer forming, siphon off and bottle. Leave for one year before opening.

PRIMROSES - Primula vulgaris

The leaves of the primrose can be used in salads. The flowers are also edible and you could scatter a few on a salad or decorate a sponge cake with them.

COWSLIPS - **Primula veris**

The word cowslip comes from cow-slop from the Old English for a cowpat and strangely cowslips grow particularly well where there are cows grazing. They are common in the South mostly in grassland on chalk, limestone or clay. They flower in April and May and have a honey smell. The flowers grow in umbels on long stems and look like drooping primroses. The leaves spread out at the base of the stem. The flowerheads can be eaten. You can scatter them over salads, pickle them or make wine with them but it would be an arduous job to collect enough flowerheads as these recipes, which were popular in the past, need large quantities of cowslips. In fact cowslips were such a popular ingredient in days gone by that this is probably what led to a decline in the prevalence of the flowers.

GORSE FLOWERS (gorse = **Ulex europaeus**)

Gorse grows throughout Britain and the flowers can be used to make wine or tea. Gorse produces a mass of bright yellow flowers from March to June and grows in grassy places and on the edges of heaths. To make tea put two handfuls of bruised gorse flowers in a mug and pour in some boiling water. Leave to infuse for 10 minutes and then strain. You can sweeten the tea with honey. For gorse flower wine follow the directions for coltsfoot wine on page 27.

BROOM - **Sarothamnus scoparius or Cystisus scoparius**

Broom is a native shrub which is common on heaths and wasteland, particularly where the soil is sandy. The leaves are oval and bunched in groups of three. Flowers are bright yellow and should be picked when still in bud any time from March but can be picked in April and May too. Broom buds can be added to salads or pickled. When the flowers are fully out they can be picked and used to make wine (see coltsfoot wine on page 24) or beer. Brooms apparently used to be made from the shrub hence its name. Do not confuse with Spanish broom which has narrow pine needle type leaves and poisonous flowers blooming later from June to August. Broom can be bought as seed from herb catalogues.

Wild Greens

WILD GARLIC Also known as Ramsons - Allium ursinum

Wild garlic's Latin name is Bear's Garlic – presumably because bears like wild garlic! It is widespread in the spring and best from March when you will see the green, quite broad, spear-shaped leaves sticking up. The flowers will be evident in April, dying away in early May, and the whole plant goes yellow and dies away in June. Wild garlic is found in damp places, in woods and under hedges. It is an attractive plant with clusters of white, star-like flowers and lily-of-the-valley leaves. You will know when you have found ramsons because they have a strong smell of garlic, especially as you pick the leaves. However as you cook them they will lose some of their pungency and the leaves will just add a mild flavour of garlic to your dish. The flowers are edible and look good added to a salad. The bulbs can be used to as a mild alternative to cloves of garlic. There is also another plant, crow garlic (allium vineale) which is common in arable fields and on roadside verges; it is more like cultivated garlic with clusters of bulbils at the top of the stems which you can pick – it has flattish leaves and rosy flowerheads and is around from June onwards. Wild garlic can be bought as seed from herb catalogues. It can be added to soups, stews and casseroles for a mild garlic flavour or used to make green garlic butter - see over the page.

Alternatively chop up some garlic leaves instead of garlic when making home-made hummus. Try snipping up some leaves and adding them to beaten eggs when making an omelette.

WILD GARLIC BUTTER

This can be added to mashed potato or used to make garlic bread.

Handful of wild garlic leaves, chopped in the food processor
75g, 3oz salted butter, softened
2 tsp lemon juice

Mash the leaves and butter together and beat in the lemon juice. Either use straightaway or roll into a sausage shape, wrap in clingfilm and store in the fridge or freezer. If using straightaway, then spread on the split slices of a granary baton, wrap in foil and put in a medium oven for 20 minutes – this makes a deliciously unusual garlic bread.

WILD GARLIC AND NETTLE SOUP
Serves 4 – 6

2 tbsp olive oil
1 onion, peeled and sliced
1 medium potato, peeled and sliced
100g, 4oz young nettle tops
100g, 4oz wild garlic
900ml, 1½pts Marigold Swiss vegetable bouillon stock
2 tbsp double cream
chopped wild garlic leaves for garnish

Heat the oil in a large saucepan and add the onion and potato and fry until softened. Add the nettles and wild garlic and stir around for a couple of minutes. Add the stock, bring to the boil, and then simmer covered for about 20 minutes. Purée the soup. Stir in the double cream, reheat if necessary and add the chopped garlic leaves.

GARLIC MUSTARD Also known as Hedge garlic or Jack-by-the-Hedge - Alliaria petiolata

This is a biennial herb, which grows in hedgerows, roadside verges, on the edges of woods and in shady gardens. It flowers from April to June. Pick the leaves in March and April when they are young and flavoursome. The jagged leaves smell of garlic when crushed and can be used in salads or for flavouring stews. You can also use it chopped up to make a garlicky herb butter similar to the wild garlic butter. Some find the leaves bitter but after rain the leaves become less bitter. In Wales garlic mustard is traditionally eaten with bacon and herrings. Seeds can be bought from herb catalogues.

DANDELION - Taraxacum officinalis

The word dandelion comes from the French for lion's tooth, probably because the jagged edges of the leaves look like lion's teeth. Dandelion leaves can be found everywhere and the young leaves in spring are best. The bitterness can be reduced if you cover the leaves with a bucket a couple of days before you pick them. Alternatively cover the leaves with a flower pot during the winter and the leaves will be very similar to endive. Pick the leaves when out for a walk, then soak them in water overnight as this improves them. They work well in conjunction with other greens. Cook some dandelion leaves in a little butter and water, adding spinach after 3 or 4 minutes and when the spinach has wilted, mix the two together and serve. They are good in salads, mixed with other leaves. You could also add them to nettle tops and make soup. Dandelion roots are edible and used in a variety of ways. They can be dug up in spring and used to make dandelion beer but are probably at their best in the autumn when they can be used to make dandelion coffee (see page 160).

DANDELION AND BACON SALAD
Serves 2 – 3

225g, 8oz young dandelion leaves mixed with other lettuce
100g, 4oz smoked streaky bacon, cooked and chopped
2 slices of bread, sliced and fried in oil to make croutons
2 hard boiled eggs, peeled and sliced
3 tbsp vinaigrette

Arrange the dandelion and other lettuce leaves in a bowl. Sprinkle the bacon and croutons over them and arrange the eggs on top. Dress with the vinaigrette and serve at once.

DANDELION BEER

Dandelion beer is a rustic, quite rough but tasty springtime homebrew. This was the favourite drink of the workmen in iron foundries and potteries of industrial towns in the Midlands.

225g, 8oz dandelion plants
4 litres, 8pts water
15g, ½oz root ginger, peeled and bruised
peel and juice of 1 lemon
450g, 1lb demerara sugar
25g, 1oz cream of tartar
25g, 1oz yeast

Use the roots and the leaves of the dandelion plants, discarding the flower stems. Wash the roots and remove any hairs from the main tap root. Chop the roots and leaves and then boil in

32

the water with the ginger and lemon rind for 10 minutes. Strain and add the sugar and cream of tartar – pour into a fermentation jar. When cooled add the lemon juice and yeast, cover and leave in a warm place for 3 days. If you don't have a fermenting vessel, use a large jug and cover with a clean towel. It will fizz but just leave it. Strain and pour into sterilised bottles, storing the bottles on their sides. Leave for a week when the beer should have cleared and it will hiss when the stopper is loosened. Drink as soon as possible as it doesn't keep for long.

DANDELION FLOWER WINE

Traditionally flowers are collected on St George's Day, 23rd April to make dandelion wine.

4 litres, 8pts dandelion flowers
4 litres, 8pts boiling water
peel of 1 orange and 1 lemon
15g, ½oz root ginger, bruised
225g, 8oz raisins, chopped
1.8kg, 4lb demerara sugar
180ml, 6fl oz cold tea
4 tsp dried yeast

Put the dandelion flowers in a container, steep them in boiling water and leave for 2 days. Then strain off the flowers and add the peel from the orange and lemon, the ginger, raisins and sugar. Heat slowly until the sugar has dissolved. Cool and add the tea and yeast. Pour into a glass jar or cask. Stand on a tray and keep in a warm room. After a while fermentation will start and froth will pour over the side of the container. When the frothing has stopped cork or insert an air lock. When fermentation is complete, ie. gas bubbles are no longer forming, siphon off and bottle.

NETTLES - **Urtica dioica**

Nettles, which are perennial herbs, can be found everywhere!! Both stinging nettles and red and white dead-nettles can be used in cooking. Young nettle shoots can be gathered in March and April and used to make nettle soup. Wear gloves (obviously) and cut the tops off with scissors. Don't pick them from June onwards as the plants become tough and bitter. Nettles flower from May to October but the flowers are minute. You may hate nettles, but apparently they are the only food for caterpillars which become peacock butterflies. Nettles were long ago known as poverty food. There is an Irish legend that St Columcille asked an old woman why she was cutting nettles. She replied that she had nothing else to eat while waiting for her cow to have its calf and come into milk. Columcille decided to live on nettle soup, while he waited for the kingdom of heaven – losing flesh 'till the track of his ribs used to be seen on the strand when he used to lie out there through the night'.

Did you know that on June 21 there is a nettle-eating competition held at the Bottle Inn in Dorset with the winner, to date, eating 56 feet of nettles (foot-long nettles are supplied)? This competition dates back to a dispute between farmers over whose nettles were the tallest. At first this was the 'longest stinging nettle competition'. Alex Williams came along with a 15ft, 6in nettle and said 'if anyone can beat that, I will eat it'. An American couple arrived with a 16ft nettle so Alex had to eat it - after that, traditionally, if Alex didn't win, he ate the winner's nettle. In 1997 the competition developed into the World Stinging Nettle Eating Challenge.

Stinging nettles are a rich source of vitamins A and C. The sting in the hairs is produced by the presence of formic acid but is destroyed, you will be pleased to know, immediately by washing or boiling. Nettles are a powerful diuretic (ie promote the discharge of urine) and were used in the past to alleviate the symptoms of urinary infections. Nettles have a salty flavour. Try also the nettle beer included below. We have tried them cooked as spinach but were not as impressed as we were with the soup.

NETTLE AND POTATO SOUP
Serves 4 – 6

1 onion, peeled and sliced
1 garlic clove, peeled and chopped
2 medium potatoes, peeled and sliced
50g, 2oz butter
175g, 6oz young nettles (use the nettle tops, stalks removed)
600ml, 1pt Marigold Swiss vegetable bouillon stock
salt and pepper
crème fraîche and croutons to serve

Fry the onion, garlic and potatoes in the butter gently for about 10 minutes. Add the nettle tops and the stock. Cover and simmer for 20 minutes. Liquidise the soup until smooth. Return to the pan and add salt and pepper. Reheat gently. Serve with small dollops of crème fraîche added to each portion and croutons.

NETTLE TEA

Simmer 25g, 1oz of nettle tops in water for 5 minutes. Strain, add the juice of half a lemon and a little honey. Alternatively you can use dried leaves - steep two teaspoons in boiling water for 10 minutes.

NETTLE BEER

1kg, 2lb young nettles
pared lemon peel and juice of 2 lemons
450g, 1lb demerara sugar
4 litres, 8pts water
25g, 1oz cream of tartar
25g, 1oz yeast

Wash the nettles and then boil in the water for 15 minutes. Strain into a bowl containing the lemon peel, juice, sugar and cream of tartar. Stir and when cool, add the yeast. Keep covered with a thick cloth for three days. Strain and bottle it. The beer will be ready to drink in eight days.

ALEXANDERS Also known as Black Lovage
Smyrnium olustratum

This is a biennial herb but was originally introduced by the Romans as a culinary plant and is a cross between parsley and celery; it's a member of the umbelliferae family. It took its name from Alexander the Great, a native of Macedonia where the plants were common. Alexanders are found in greatest profusion within a few miles of the sea in hedgerows, on roadside verges, wasteland or patches of grassland. Sometimes Alexanders can be found further inland close to monastic sites where they were once cultivated. They were grown in kitchen gardens and known as Alexandrian parsley. Alexanders are around much of the year with leaves appearing in January. Several parts of the plant can be used – the young leaves which are toothed and glossy, can be used in salads in early spring. The greenish-yellow flowers which appear in the spring can be used in salads or to make fritters. They taste spicy and slightly peppery. The roots can also be used as a vegetable, cooked in the same way as parsnips. The stems, however, are the best bit and they should be used in April and May. Take the young stems off the central stem. Strip off the leaves, peel the central, thick, hollow stem which is pinkish in colour and take off about ¼in, 5mm to remove all the stringy outer covering. Cut into smaller lengths. You can also use the stems which branch off the outer stem but you will need to peel them as well. My mistake when first using Alexanders was not to peel them (some books do not mention that Alexanders stems need to be peeled) and then you end up with very stringy, inedible stalks. Boil as you would asparagus in salted water for between 8 and 10 minutes. Eat them like asparagus seasoned with melted butter. Alexanders are similar to wild angelica or wild celery – they do have a celery-like smell. The black fruit or seeds appear later on in the year and can be ground as you would peppercorns. Alexanders seeds can be bought from the Suffolk Herbs catalogue.

ALEXANDERS IN MADEIRA CREAM SAUCE
Serves 4

450g, 1lb Alexanders stems, peeled to remove outer layer
and cut into 7.5cm, 3in lengths
25g, 1oz butter
1 tbsp olive oil
1 onion, peeled and chopped
1 garlic clove, peeled and crushed
4 tbsp Marigold Swiss vegetable bouillon stock
1 tbsp plain flour
4 tbsp Madeira
1 egg yolk

Heat the butter and oil in a pan and add the onion and garlic. Sauté until softened, then add the stems and stock, cover and simmer for 10 minutes. Mix the flour with the Madeira and a little water. Add this paste into the pan and cook, stirring until the sauce is smooth. Remove from the heat and stir in the yolk. Add seasoning and serve as a vegetable side dish.

HOP SHOOTS - **Humulus lupulus**

Hops are grown commercially in Kent for the making of beer but you can also eat them. They will be abundant in areas where they are being grown for beer, probably because they have escaped from cultivation. The hop is a perennial which will die right back in the winter and appear again in the spring, climbing around other bushes in the hedgerows. The plants have toothed leaves like ivy but are paler green. The female flowers grow into cone-shaped green heads which are the part used to flavour beer. The male flowers are branched catkins and these are the shoots to pick. Hop shoots were eaten by the Romans, as mentioned by the Roman author, Pliny. Pick the small, young, red-tinged shoots in March and April. They should be rinsed, tied together like asparagus and boiled in salted water for a few minutes. Eat them like asparagus with melted butter. You can also make tea with the leaves of hops.

FAT HEN Also known as White Goosefoot - Chenpodium album and GOOD KING HENRY - Chenopodium bonus henricus

Fat hen is a native annual with deep green diamond or lance shaped leaves – it grows all over Britain as a weed on bare soil and waste ground. It can reach 1.5m, 5ft high in mid summer. The alternative name 'goosefoot' from the Latin, is easy to understand when you look at the web-foot-like formation of the leaves. Good King Henry is a perennial which looks very similar to fat hen - it's known as mercury in the wild. It can be bought as a plant or as seed and added to your herb garden. It will reseed itself. Both are rich in vitamin B1, iron, calcium and are higher in protein than cabbage or spinach. They can be cooked like spinach, eaten in salads or used in soup. The seeds, in times gone by, were harvested and ground into flour for making bread – they are apparently like buckwheat in flavour.

You can also pick the flowering spikes of good King Henry, ready in June, and steam them like broccoli, serving them with melted butter.

FAT HEN SOUP
Serves 2 – 3

1 onion, peeled and sliced
2 tbsp olive oil
1 clove of garlic, peeled and crushed
handful of fat hen or good King Henry leaves
600ml, 1pt Marigold Swiss vegetable bouillon stock
50g, 2oz rice, cooked

Sauté the onion in the olive oil with the garlic. Add the fat hen leaves and then the stock. Allow to simmer for 15 minutes, adding the rice for the last 5 minutes.

FAT HEN AND POTATO LAYERED PIE
Serves 4 as a side dish

2 or 3 handfuls of fat hen, blanched and chopped
450g, 1lb potatoes, peeled and sliced
50g, 2oz butter
1 small tin of anchovies, chopped
50g, 2oz gruyere cheese
25g, 1oz breadcrumbs

Lay the fat hen in a greased baking dish. Cover with a layer of potatoes and dot them with butter. Cover with more fat hen and another layer of potatoes and spread the anchovies over the top. Add another layer of fat hen and sprinkle the breadcrumbs and cheese and a little more butter over the top. Bake in the oven at gas mark 4, 180°C (350°F) for 25 minutes.

GROUND ELDER Also known as Bishop's weed or Goutweed - Aegopodium podagraria

This is a perennial and usually regarded as an invasive weed since the roots spread relentlessly. Not everyone realises it makes a tasty green vegetable. It grows everywhere in gardens, on waste ground, on roadsides and under hedges. Once ground elder was cultivated as a pot herb! The Romans introduced it to Britain and used it to cure gout. Although no relation to the elder tree, the leaves are similar in shape and hence the name. Gather the young bright green, sharply toothed, oval leaves in early spring. You can run cold water over them but don't soak in water as this stains the leaves. Cook until tender in salted boiling water or cook in butter with a little water for about 10 minutes, stirring as you go – in other words, cook as you would spinach. If you let it grow on, white flowers appear in June on top of hairless stalks and these are followed by egg-shaped fruits. Ground elder has a tangy, aromatic, parsley-like flavour.

GROUND ELDER IN TOMATO SAUCE
Serves 4 as a vegetable side dish

3 handfuls of young ground elder leaves
1 onion, peeled and chopped
25g, 1oz butter
25g, 1oz plain flour
150ml, ¼pt Marigold Swiss vegetable bouillon stock
2 tsp tomato purée

Fry the onion in the butter until softened. Add the flour and then gradually add the stock and stir until you have a smooth sauce. Mix in the tomato purée. Throw in the ground elder and stir to heat through.

GROUND ELDER PESTO

This has a pleasant flavour and is quite a clever way of using up an unwanted weed.

> *2 handfuls ground elder leaves, unwashed*
> *2 cloves of garlic, peeled and crushed*
> *50g, 2oz walnuts*
> *8 tbsp olive oil*
> *2 tbsp grated Parmesan or mature Cheddar cheese*

Put the elder leaves in the food processor and add the garlic and walnuts. Process briefly and then gradually add the olive oil with the motor still running. Lastly add the Parmesan. Use as a sauce for pasta, serve with fish or mix into a potato salad with some boiled eggs.

LUNGWORT - Pulmonaria officinalis

Apparently lungwort is named because the white-spotted leaves look like human lungs. It was also thought that the plant could cure respiratory diseases such as TB and pneumonia. The plant grows up to 30cm, 1ft high in woods and hedgerows. The flowers are pink at first and then turn blue. You can use the leaves as a green vegetable.

GOLDEN SAXIFRAGE
Chrysosplenium oppositifolium

This is a small plant found in wet, shady places which forms a thick mat of rooting stems. Golden saxifrage is fairly common in the North and West and in Wiltshire is called buttered eggs. The leaves grow as a rosette beneath groups of petal-less flowers. They can be used as a green vegetable and cooked as you would spinach.

LADY'S SMOCK Also known as Cuckoo Flower
Cardamine pratensis

Lady's smock is a hairless perennial and a member of the bittercress family. From a rosette at the base root, leaves grow in opposite pairs. White or pale lilac flowers appear in April – at the time the cuckoo is first heard – hence its alternative name. It is common in damp meadows, ditches and near the edges of water. Use the leaves in salads: it has a taste similar to watercress. This is the favourite plant of the orange tip butterfly.

SORREL - Rumex

There are various sorts of sorrel. Common or garden sorrel (rumex acetosa) can also be called broad leaf sorrel – this is widespread in woods and meadows and along roadside verges. Sheep sorrel (rumex acetosella) is similar but has smaller leaves – it also grows everywhere but not on chalky soils. French sorrel (rumex scutatus) is also known as buckler leaf sorrel. This is a cultivated variety – the leaves are less acid and it is used to make the famous French sorrel soup. Finally there is wood sorrel (oxalis acetosella) – this is a small, delicate perennial plant with lime green leaves and small white flowers – as the name suggests it is found in woodland and leaves can be picked in the early spring.

All sorrel leaves are rich in vitamin C, oxalic and other acids and rich in iron. The young leaves only should be picked and used in mixed salads or chopped up and added to an omelette.

SORREL AND PEA SOUP
Serves 8

1 tbsp olive oil
1 onion, peeled and chopped
bunch of French sorrel, about 12 large leaves
1.5 litres, 2½pts chicken stock
450g, 1lb fresh or frozen peas
salt and pepper
grated rind of 1 lemon

Heat the oil in a large saucepan and cook the onion until soft. Add the sorrel leaves and stir until they are soft. Add the stock and bring to the boil. Add the peas, salt and pepper and simmer for 15 minutes. Purée and sieve the soup. Return to a clean saucepan, heat through and add the grated lemon rind.

BEECH LEAVES (beech = fagus sylvatica)

Young beech leaves, picked in April, can be added to salads. They have a cabbagey flavour.

NOYAU

Beech leaves
1 bottle of gin
sugar
dash of brandy or sherry

Pack a glass or earthenware jar full of beech leaves. Pour a bottle of gin over them and press them down - the leaves will lose their bright green colour. Leave to infuse for 2 weeks. Strain off the gin which will now be a greeny yellow colour. For every 600ml, 1pt of gin, use 350g, 12oz of sugar and dissolve it in 300ml, ½pt of boiling water. Add to the gin with a dash of brandy and bottle when cold.

OTHER EDIBLE WEEDS – PLANTAIN is a perennial weed. Like the other weeds already mentioned, plantain leaves should be gathered when young and make a good spinach-like vegetable but must be well cooked. **CHARLOCK** is a weed with bright yellow flowers. Its seeds can remain buried for as long as 50 years and it still germinates in farmers' fields. Charlock has cabbage like leaves and is found on arable fields and on roadside verges. Pick young leaves and cook as for spinach.

Wild herbs

COW PARSLEY or WILD CHERVIL
Also known as Queen Anne's Lace – Anthiscus sylvestris

Cow parsley flowers from April to June and is one of the commonest early flowering plants. This biennial wild herb is abundant on roadside verges, in hedgerows and edges of woods all over Britain. It is a leafy branched plant growing to about 1m, 3ft tall with green, hollowed, furrowed stems which are hairy near the base. Leaves resemble wedge-shaped ferns and flowers are tiny white umbels. Cow parsley can be confused with poisonous species such as fool's parsley (much smaller with thin, hairless, ribbed stems and darker, cream flowers) and hemlock (purple spotted stems and only grows near water) so pick when stems are developed and you can positively identify it. In the past children used to use the hollowed stems as pea shooters. Cow parsley is best used as a herb and has a flavour like cultivated chervil. Don't cook it, though, as it loses its flavour. You can chop it up and add to a potato salad or add a little to a salad of mixed leaves.

HOGWEED Also known as Cow Parsnip
Heracleum sphondylium

Hogweed is a common biennial herb which is abundant in hedges, waste ground and grassy places, usually hiding amongst the grass, nettles and dock leaves, in most of Britain, but not so much in the far North. It is a member of the celery family (umbelliferae) but tastes nothing like celery. The young stems are fleshy and at their best in April before the plant starts flowering. Pick them before the leaves have fully uncurled. The stems are hairy, slightly bristly, grooved and hollow. Wash them and cook with a little butter and water until tender. Serve with a little more butter and a sprinkling of lemon juice. According to some books these are one of the tastiest wild vegetables, but my family disagreed. They have quite a strange taste. Hogweed flowers from May to October and can grow up to 2m, 6ft tall. Do not confuse with giant hogweed which can grow much taller, up to 5m, 15ft and has thick red blotched stems.

COMFREY Also known as Wound wort
Symphytum officinale

Comfrey is a perennial, evergreen herb that can often be seen along river banks and roadside ditches – it especially likes damp places. Only the young leaves (these have a rough texture and sticky feel to them) should be picked, any time from April. Comfrey flowers from May to October and the bell-shaped flowers can be white, pink or purple. The leaves can be used in the form of fomentations for sprains and bruises. Comfrey is also used as an expectorant for catarrhal congestion and to soothe intestinal troubles. Cook the leaves as you would spinach. Comfrey is the only vegetable to contain vitamin B12. It also has a higher protein content than any other green vegetable except the soya bean. Tea can be made from dried comfrey leaves. Pick the leaves before midday, spread them flat on racks in an airy place. When brittle, crumble them up and pack into airtight containers. Comfrey stems can be cooked like asparagus. You can grow comfrey in your garden but once you have planted it, like mint, majoram and Jerusalem artichokes, it will be almost impossible to get rid of – it has persistent, deeply penetrating roots. These roots, glutinous and slimy, used to be dug up in March, grated and used as plaster to set broken limbs – the slowly setting mash acted as a healing poultice for compound fractures. In Scotland it was known as boneset.

If you plant seeds in spring, by the summer the comfrey will have grown and spread considerably – the outside leaves grow up to about 60cm, 2ft long and the plant up to 1m, 3ft tall so you will need to keep it in check. Comfrey makes a great liquid feed or add to your compost heap as an activator.

COMFREY FRITTERS
Serves 4

2 handfuls of comfrey leaves

For the batter
100g, 4oz plain flour
150ml, ¼pt milk or water
1 egg

Strip the leaves off the plant and dip them in cold water. To make the batter, tip the flour into a bowl and make a well in the centre. Gradually beat in the egg and milk. Take two or three leaves of similar size, place them together and dip in the batter. Deep fry them in oil until golden on both sides.

HERB BENNET
Also known as Wood Avens - Geum urbanum

Herb bennet is common in woodlands and shaded hedgerows – it likes damp places. Dig up the roots in spring – they smell like cloves and can be used to flavour soups and stews. One handful of roots is equivalent to one clove. Yellow five petalled flowers appear in May. The young leaves can also be used in salads. Dried roots put amongst your clothes are supposed to keep the moths away.

WILD CHIVES - Allium schoenoprasum

Chives are quite common on roadside verges and in country lanes, perhaps as escapees from cultivated herb gardens. One of the most useful herbs, you can add them as a garnish to soups, casseroles and sauces.

LEMON BALM - Melissa officinalis

The Greeks believed this herb very important medicinally and it was sacred to the Temple of Diana - lemon balm tea is meant to be a great pick-me-up. Beekeepers plant the herb near their hives as the flowers are rich in nectar. In the past it was grown in gardens for its sweet lemon-scented leaves and flowers and spread to roadside verges. There is a pretty variegated lemon balm that you can plant in your garden - balm will spread and the leaves can be used in dishes or salads for a lemon flavour.

Mushrooms

ST GEORGE'S MUSHROOMS
Tricholoma gambosum

These mushrooms are so called after St George's Day on 23rd April as this was often when they would first be seen growing in fairy rings in the grass. They are pale creamy white to buff colour with a fleshy cap up to 15cm, 6in across and short thick stems, swollen at the base. They can be found in thick, grassy places in chalky fields or on open downs, in open, grassy woods or sometimes in orchards. St George's mushrooms are good fried but toughen if cooked in casseroles. Use them as you would cultivated mushrooms.

ROASTED MUSHROOMS ON TOAST
Serves 4 as a starter

8 St George's mushrooms
3 tbsp olive oil
2 cloves of garlic, peeled and chopped
50g, 2oz butter
1 tsp horseradish cream
4 slices of toast
fresh parsley for garnish

Brush the mushrooms with olive oil and place on a baking tray with the garlic scattered over them. Put in the oven at gas mark 4, 180°C (350°F) for 20 minutes, basting them with oil after 10 minutes. Mix the butter and horseradish and spread over the toast. Top each with two mushrooms and sprinkle parsley over the top.

MUSHROOM AND SORREL FILLED
CHEESE PANCAKES
Serves 4 – 6

For the batter
300ml, ½pt milk
1 egg
100g, 4oz plain flour

450g, 1lb St George's mushrooms, chopped
1 onion, peeled and sliced
25g, 1oz butter
50g, 2oz sorrel leaves, chopped
50g, 2oz mature Cheddar cheese, grated

Make the batter by combining all the ingredients in a food processor. Cook 6 - 8 pancakes. Melt the butter in a frying pan and sauté the mushrooms and onion for a few minutes - allow the juices to evaporate. Add the yoghurt and simmer gently without allowing to boil. Mix in the sorrel and let it wilt over the heat for a couple of minutes. Fill each pancake with a spoonful of mixture. Roll up and transfer to an ovenproof dish. Scatter with cheese and cook in the oven at gas mark 4, 180°C (350°F), for 15 minutes.

MORELS - Morchella esculenta

Morels are spring fungi – they have a rounded, conical cap covered with sharp ridges, irregularly arranged like honeycomb or a sponge. Colour varies from pale yellowish brown to blackish-grey. Morels grow under leafy trees, in hedgerows, on banks and damp meadows, often on sandy soils overlying chalk. To prepare, cut in half and make sure there are no insects lurking inside the holes. Remove the base of the stem. Wash under a cold tap and then drop into boiling water to blanch for a few seconds. Morels are excellent for drying. After washing them thread onto string and hang up in a warm kitchen or by a radiator – when they are dry and crisp pack into a jar. To rehydrate, soak in water for 30 minutes. Morels provide good flavouring for stews, soups and sauces. Since they are hollow, they make good stuffed mushrooms.

MORELS STUFFED WITH SCRAMBLED EGGS
Serves 2

4 morels
3 eggs, scrambled
a little butter
wild herbs

Cook the morels in salted boiling water for 5 minutes. Rinse them in cold water and cut them down the stalk and across the cap. Gently fry them in a little butter, fill the hollows with scrambled eggs and serve on toast if liked.

FRENCH ONION AND MOREL SOUP
Serves 4

50g, 2oz butter
3 onions, peeled and sliced
900ml, 1½pts beef stock
4 tbsp sherry
225g, 8oz morels
4 slices of toasted cheese

Melt the butter in a saucepan and sauté the onion. Add the beef stock, sherry and morels. Cover and simmer for 20 minutes. Divide the soup between four bowls and top with toasted cheese.

On the Sea Shore

SEA KALE or SEA CABBAGE - Crambe maritima

This is a native perennial found on Britain's coasts on sand, shingle, rock and cliff faces. You can pick it in April when other green vegetables are sparse. Sea kale is particularly prevalent in the pebbles which are often covered by water in the high spring tides. The plant produces white clusters of flowers from June to August. The Romans used to pick sea kale and keep it in barrels to use on sea voyages. It looks like cabbage and grows in clumps with grey-green leaves. It is the shoots that you eat as well as the leaves which you can use like spinach. To cook, cut the stems so that they are equal lengths and tie them in a bundle before boiling in water until tender and serve as you would asparagus with melted butter. Sea kale can also be cultivated in your garden. You can either buy some seeds or use seeds from the plants collected at the beach. After the plants have flowered, around September they will produce dark-grey seed pods. You need to break off the outer casing and retrieve the seed inside which is about the size of a grape pip. Keep these until the following spring and then grow in small pots. Prick out the seedlings and transfer to larger pots – plant them out in July about 1m, 3ft apart. Like asparagus you shouldn't use the shoots for the first two seasons. In the following spring cover the crowns with straw and place forcing jars or upturned buckets over the plants. The blanched stems will sprout – you can cut these off when they are about 20cm, 8in long and new shoots will grow over the next three weeks. When leaves start to appear remove the jars or buckets. Sea kale, like rhubarb and asparagus, will go on producing shoots for at least 10 years.

SEA BEET - Beta maritima

This is also known as sea spinach and is a perennial which can grow up to 1m, 3ft high. It is found along the coasts of Britain on dunes, cliffs and shingle but is rare in Scotland. The leaves are dark green, shiny and spear-shaped towards the top. They can be picked from April for most of the year. In May the plants produce long spikes of small green flowers with yellow anthers. Sea beet is a wild species of cultivated beet like spinach. Use the leaves as you would spinach but wash them well to get rid of the salty taste.

LATE SPRING
May

By this time the sun should be warming the ground up and there should be no more frosts. You can plant out broccoli, and Brussels sprouts seedlings, courgette and tomato plants, squash and pumpkin plants, outdoor cucumbers, French and runner beans, leeks and turnips. Continue to sow salad leaves. By now you should be able to pick radishes, spinach, salad leaves and rocket. Other than that you can forage for some exciting wild greens. You can gather hawthorn leaves and blossom, goat's beard, woodruff, red valerian, nipplewort, hawkbit, scurvy grass, wild fennel, brooklime, lime leaves and flowers, ground ivy and tansy. Other plants such as Alexanders, dandelions, sorrels and chickweed will all still be flourishing; also yarrow which can be gathered from May right the way through to January. The first cultivated fruits of the year are gooseberries. If you have gooseberry bushes you should be able to pick these from mid May. Fairy ring mushrooms should also appear, providing there has been some rain and on the coasts you should start finding rock samphire and sea beet will still be prolific.

CULTIVATED VEGETABLES

RADISHES - Raphanus sativus

Radishes are one of the oldest vegetables and thought to be native to China. They spread to the Mediterranean and were much used by the Romans, Greeks and Egyptians. The Roman writer, Pliny describes the radish as 'having a remarkable power of causing flatulence and belching and consequently a vulgar part of the diet.' They are one of the easiest vegetables to grow but not particularly versatile. They're good eaten fresh on their own or in a salad. As soon as possible in the early spring you can plant radish seeds. Radishes grow quickly so they make a useful vegetable to grow in between parsnip and carrot seeds which take a long time to germinate. In this way you will know where you have planted your main crop and you can pick the radishes well before the parsnips and carrots have developed fully. Beware of sowing seeds too late in the season as the radishes will bolt in hot weather.

Radishes contain vitamins B and C. The bite or tanginess that you can taste in a radish is due to the presence of mustard oil. Radishes are usually red but you can also get black, purple, yellow and green-skinned types. The most popular traditional varieties are red such as Cherry Belle and Scarlet Globe. For fun you may want to make radish flowers – to do this cut off the root but leave a little bit of the green tip. Make about six to eight cuts from the stalk end in the radish and then leave in iced water for at least an hour – the radish will have curled out where you made the slits in the form of a flower.

RADISH AND MANGO SALAD
Serves 4

1 mango, peeled and diced
100g, 4oz radishes, topped, tailed and sliced
3 tbsp olive oil
1 tbsp lemon juice
few drops of tabasco sauce
½ tsp dried chilli flakes
2 tbsp chopped fresh coriander leaves

Place the mango and sliced radishes in a bowl. Mix together the oil, lemon juice and tabasco sauce and pour over the mango and radishes. Sprinkle the chilli flakes and coriander over the top and serve.

SPINACH - **Spinacia olearica**

Spinach originated in Persia – the word comes from a Persian word, aspanakh. It was first cultivated for its medicinal properties. The Arabs introduced it to Europe in the thirteenth century but it wasn't introduced to Britain until the 1500s. Spinach did not arrive in America until the nineteenth century when there is evidence that Thomas Jefferson was growing it in his garden.

There are two types of true spinach - summer spinach which has smooth round seeds - types to be recommended are Monnopa, Medania, Trinidad and Bordeaux F1 which has red-veined leaves. The hardier prickly-seeded variety is grown for winter use.

The other three varieties that resemble spinach but are not true types are New Zealand spinach which is a creeping, spreading plant – it is also known as cut and come again spinach. This spinach lasts well through the summer and does not bolt to seed in hot weather like summer spinach. The other two types are seakale beet or Swiss chard which are included on page 164 along with winter spinach and spinach beet or perpetual spinach which can be grown at any time.

Seeds for summer spinach, New Zealand and perpetual spinach can be sown in March and April. You should be able to harvest summer spinach in May and June. If you are going to grow spinach you need to devote a decent amount of space to it – you need to harvest a lot of spinach at once as it cooks down to a much smaller amount. Spinach is very high in iron, calcium and Vitamin A but also contains oxalic acid. It contains folate, a B vitamin that helps prevent heart disease and lutein which helps prevent age-related loss of eyesight.

SPINACH, EGG AND HAM PIE
Serves 6

250g, 9oz shortcrust pastry
1 onion, peeled and sliced
1 clove of garlic, peeled and crushed
2 tbsp olive oil
275g, 10oz spinach
225g, 8oz sliced ham
225g, 8oz mozzarella cheese, sliced
1 red pepper, deseeded and chopped
4 eggs, beaten

Roll the pastry into two rounds, one slightly bigger than the other. Line a greased 20cm, 8in pie dish with the bigger round and keep the other round for the lid. Sauté the onion and garlic in the oil. Cook the spinach for a few minutes in a little water and then drain and chop it before stirring it into the onion mixture. Lay slices of ham on the pastry base. Cover with the mozzarella. Lay the spinach mixture on top and sprinkle on the chopped red pepper. Pour the beaten eggs over the top reserving a little. Cover with the pastry lid, brush with the reserved egg and cut slits in the pastry. Bake in the oven at gas mark 6, 200°C (400°F) for 35 minutes, or until golden on top.

SPINACH ROULADE
Serves 3 - 4

675g, 1½lb fresh spinach, washed
4 eggs, separated
pinch of nutmeg

Cheese sauce
40g, 1½oz butter
25g, 1oz plain flour
300ml, ½pt milk
100g, 4oz mature Cheddar cheese, grated
cayenne pepper

To make the roulade, cook the spinach without any water in a covered saucepan for a few minutes. Drain off any liquid that has formed and chop finely. Mix the egg yolks with the spinach and season with nutmeg. Whisk the egg whites until they form soft peaks. Stir one tablespoon of egg white into the spinach mixture and then fold in the rest in two batches. Pour this mixture into a lined, greased Swiss roll tin and bake in the oven at gas mark 6, 200°C (400°F) for 10 minutes. Turn the roulade out onto a clean sheet of greaseproof paper and peel off the lining paper. Make the cheese sauce by melting the butter, stirring in the flour and gradually adding the milk. Stir until smooth and mix in half the grated cheese. Spread some of the cheese sauce over the roulade and roll up carefully. Don't worry if it cracks a little – this is normal. Pour the remaining cheese sauce over the top and sprinkle with the remaining grated cheese and a little cayenne pepper. Return to the oven for 5 minutes so that the cheese melts. Serve immediately.

SPINACH SOUFFLÉ
Serves 3 – 4

225g, 8oz spinach leaves
50g, 2oz butter
1 tbsp flour
150ml, ¼pt milk
4 eggs, separated
25g, 1oz mature Cheddar cheese, grated

Wash the spinach and cook it with no extra liquid in a saucepan for about 3 minutes. Drain it well and squeeze out any extra liquid. Chop it finely and cook briefly in half the butter. Melt the remaining butter in a saucepan and add the flour. Gradually add the milk and make up a white sauce. Remove from the heat and add the egg yolks. Beat in the grated cheese and then mix in the spinach. Beat the egg whites until stiff and fold these in. Spoon into a soufflé dish and bake in the oven at gas mark 5, 190°C (375°F) for about 25 minutes or until well risen.

ROCKET - Eruca sativa

Rocket is a very versatile salad plant. The leaves are spicy but can become very hot and pungent as the plants mature. It prefers to grow in cooler weather and tends to run to seed in a hot summer. Rocket can survive right through a mild winter. Sow seeds very early in the year and you will get a plentiful supply through the spring. Sow more seeds in the autumn for winter supplies. You can also leave some plants to run to seed in summer and store the seeds for sowing later. Wild rocket is also a clever plant to grow as it is a perennial so dies back in the winter, coming back in the spring. It also seems to spread quite easily so may crop up all over your vegetable border.

LINGUINE WITH ROCKET AND ANCHOVIES
Serves 4

4 slices of brown bread, crumbled
250g, 9oz linguine
4 tbsp olive oil
2 cloves of garlic, peeled and crushed
6 anchovies, drained and chopped
1 tsp dried chilli flakes
100g, 4oz rocket or wild rocket
50g, 2oz Parmesan cheese, grated

Toast the breadcrumbs under a hot grill. Cook the linguine. In the meantime heat the oil in a pan and add the garlic and anchovies. Cook for a couple of minutes and add the chilli flakes. Add the cooked pasta and add the rocket and Parmesan. Toss together and serve.

ROCKET PESTO

100g, 4oz rocket leaves
2 garlic cloves, peeled
50g, 2oz walnuts
90ml, 3fl oz olive oil
50g, 2oz Parmesan cheese, grated

Process the rocket, garlic and walnuts. Continue to process while you drizzle in the olive oil. Mix in the Parmesan cheese and serve with pasta of your choice or store and eat with cod or salmon.

CULTIVATED FRUITS

GOOSEBERRIES - Ribes grossularia

Gooseberries, native to Europe and North America, grew wild all over Britain for centuries before being cultivated in the 1500s. They became very popular after that. They are high in Vitamin C and also contain A and D, potassium, calcium, phosphorus and niacin. They would give you 17 calories per 100g. They are rich in pectin and so good for jam. They have a long season – early green gooseberries can be cooked and used in fruit fools, pies etc. They come in many varieties and range in colour from bright green to a wonderful purple. They freeze well.

MACKEREL WITH GOOSEBERRY SAUCE
Serves 4

4 fresh mackerel, filleted
2 tbsp fine oatmeal
salt and pepper
knob of butter
225g, 8oz gooseberries
1 tsp brown sugar
1 egg, beaten

Season the mackerel inside and oat with salt and pepper. Sprinkle the oatmeal evenly over the mackerel and dot with the butter. Cook under a pre-heated grill for 20 minutes. Meanwhile make the sauce. Purée and sieve the gooseberries to remove the pips. Put the purée in a small saucepan with the sugar and beat in the egg, warming gently and stirring. Place the mackerel on a warm serving dish and spoon over the sauce.

GOOSEBERRY FOOL
Serves 4 - 6

450g, 1lb gooseberries
2 tbsp water
100g, 4oz caster sugar
1 egg white
300ml, ½pt double cream

Wash the gooseberries and place in a saucepan with the water. Bring to the boil and simmer for about 10 minutes until soft. Then stir in the sugar which will dissolve. Pass the fruit through a sieve and allow the purée to cool. Whip up the cream and in a separate bowl whisk the egg white. Fold both the egg white and the cream into the gooseberry purée and chill before serving.

IN THE WILD
Wild Greens

HAWTHORN LEAVES AND BLOSSOM
(Hawthorn = Crataegus oxyacantha)

Hawthorn grows throughout Britain as part of hedges, in woods, around grassland and on roadside verges. The small, glossy green, deeply-lobed leaves can be picked in late spring but beware of the spiny branches. The leaves used to be called 'bread and cheese' (nothing to do with the taste but probably a metaphor for a basic foodstuff) and children used to eat them on the way to school. The leaves make a useful additional ingredient in a salad, go well in a potato salad or added to beetroot. Hawthorn blossoms which are usually white, sometimes pink, can be picked throughout May. These used to be used for May Day Garlands and any servant who brought in a branch of hawthorn blossom on May Day was given a bowl of cream.The blossom can be added to a wine cup or used to make Hawthorn Brandy. Fill a Kilner Jar with flowers and top up with brandy. Leave it for three weeks, then strain off the brandy and sweeten to taste with granulated sugar. Hawthorn flowers make one of the best flower wines.

HAWTHORN FLOWER WINE

2 litres, 4pts hawthorn flowers
1.5kg, 3lb granulated sugar
grated rind of 2 lemons
4 litres, 8pts water
25g, 1oz yeast

Add the grated rind, the juice and the sugar to the water and bring slowly to the boil to dissolve the sugar. Boil for 20 minutes and then cool. Add the yeast and leave for 24 hours before adding the flowers. Let the mixture stand for a week, stirring each day. Strain into a fermenting vessel and fit an air lock. Rack which means syphoning off into a clean jar. Leave for at least six months, syphon off again and bottle in the usual way.

GOAT'S BEARD Also known as Jack-go-to-bed-at-noon Trapopogon pratensis

Goat's beard grows on roadsides, rough ground and cultivated land. It is an annual or perennial and grows up to 60cm, 2ft with a long tap root. The narrow, grass-like leaves sheath the stem. It flowers in June and July and produces one single bright yellow flower which opens early and closes at noon (hence the nicknames Jack-go-to-bed-at-noon or Sleep-at-noon). Somerset people call this plant Sleepy Head or Twelve

O'clocks. The flower, a bit like a dandelion, eventually produces a fluffy 'clock' of seeds which scatter on the wind. The name goat's beard presumably refers to the long silky parachute hairs. Goat's beard is similar to salsify, which is a cultivated plant originally developed from the wild, also referred to as yellow goat's beard (see salsify on page 194). The leaves and roots of goat's beard can be eaten. The roots taste like parsnips. Peel the roots in the same way but keep them white by sprinkling with lemon juice. Use as parsnips. Use the leaves raw in salads.

WOODRUFF Also known as Kiss-Me-Quick and Ladies in the Hay - Galium odoratum

Woodruff grows all over Britain but particularly in chalky and limestone soils. It can be found in thick hedgerows and woodlands especially around beech trees. It can also be cultivated in gardens as a rock plant. Pick it when it is flowering in May and June. It grows about 30cm, 1ft tall and has smooth, squarish stems, star-like whorls of between six and nine leaves and small white four-petalled flowers. When the plants are green they do not smell. But pick the leaves, stems and flowers and allow them to dry and they will smell of freshly harvested hay. To dry the plants put the flowers, leaves and stalks in a dark, dry place on a piece of cloth and leave for a few days. Woodruff used to be used to scent bed linen. It also used to be strewn on the floors of churches to give a lovely scent when walked on. As a dried herb it can be used to flavour summer drinks or you can make tea from the dried flowers. Add a sprig of woodruff to apple juice and leave to steep for a week – it will have a delicious flavour. Gerard wrote, 'when added to a wine-cup it will make a man merrie'. Woodruff can also be used in ice cream and gives a vanilla like flavour. It has a reputation as a remedy to lift depression. The curious smell of dried woodruff is due to a substance called coumarin which apparently imparts a calming effect (medieval herbalists realised this). Coumarin was also found to have anti-coagulant qualities.

WINE AND WOODRUFF CUP

1 small handful of dried woodruff leaves
juice of 1 lemon
½ a bottle of white wine
2 tbsp granulated sugar
1 tbsp brandy
handful of strawberries

Put the woodruff leaves in a bowl and pour over the lemon juice and wine. Leave for three hours. Mix in the sugar and brandy. Serve this wine cup decorated with strawberries.

RED VALERIAN - Kentranthus ruber

This plant was introduced to Britain from Southern Europe in the sixteenth century. It now grows throughout the country in rocky places, on old walls especially in the South West. It is an attractive plant with clusters of red flowers which are actually pollinated by butterflies. Red Valerians have some interesting nicknames in the West Country, namely Drunkards, Drunken Sailors and Drunken Willies. In France and Italy the young leaves are boiled with butter or eaten raw in salads. They are probably best mixed with other salad ingredients as they have quite a bitter taste.

HAWKBIT - Leontodon hispidus

Hawkbit looks like a dandelion. A native perennial, the rough hawkbit is the one that's edible. It has single yellow flowers which open in May and flower right through until the autumn. It grows mostly in England on chalk soil, all over grassy slopes and roadside verges. You can use the leaves like dandelion in salads or as a cooked vegetable. The root can also be substituted for a dandelion root.

NIPPLEWORT - Lapsana communis

Nipplewort grows by roadsides, in woods and waste ground all over Britain. It is so called because the buds look like a woman's nipples and indeed were once used as a cure for sore nipples. The plant flowers from June to September – about 20 heads of small yellow flowers are borne on stems growing up to 1m, 3ft tall. The buds open early in the morning but close early in the afternoon and remain closed on dull days! The leaves make a good addition to salads.

SCURVY GRASS - Cochlearia officinalis and anglica

There are four types of scurvy grass - the two worth mentioning here are common scurvy grass so called because the leaves contain vitamin C and sailors suffering from scurvy sores were cured by eating the dried herbs or juice from this plant. It is common in salt marshes and on sea shores and is quite bitter to the taste. The plant has shiny round leaves and white flowers. It flowers from May to August. The long leaved scurvy grass (Cochlearia anglica) is rare but sometimes can be found on muddy shores and estuaries in the South - it is the better tasting of the two types.

WILD FENNEL - Foeniculum vulgare

This is a tall perennial which can reach 120cm, 4ft and has yellow flowerheads appearing from July through until October. Leaves can be picked from May right through until autumn. If you pick some leaves and crush them in your hand you will smell the aniseed flavour. Wild fennel is especially abundant on cliff tops around the coasts of South West England. This is a good wild herb to serve with fish and also goes well with egg dishes. The fennel seeds can be gathered later on after the plant has flowered and added to apple pies. Fennel seeds can be crushed and steeped in boiling water. Allow to cool and then use as a remedy for hiccups or indigestion.

BROOKLIME - Veronica beccabunga

This is a low creeping perennial which grows in wet places and is similar in habitat and taste to watercress. It has bright blue flowers which appear between May and September. Brooklime plants retain their leaves throughout the year so you could pick the leaves for a winter salad. But for easy identification it may be best to wait until May when the plant is flowering.

BROOKLIME SOUP
Serves 4 – 6

2 tbsp olive oil
2 cloves of garlic, peeled and crushed
pinch of dried chillies
225g, 8oz potatoes, peeled and diced
175g, 6oz brooklime leaves
1 litre, 2pts Marigold Swiss vegetable bouillon stock
3 tbsp mature Cheddar cheese, grated
3 chunks of brown bread, cubed and fried in oil to make croutons

Heat the oil in a saucepan and add the garlic, dried chillies and potatoes. After a couple of minutes add the brooklime and let it wilt down. Add the stock and simmer for 20 minutes. Divide between bowls and sprinkle grated cheese and croutons on top.

LIME LEAVES (lime = tilia vulgaris)

Lime trees can be found growing along country lanes and copses. This stately tree can also be found in parks and gardens. Pick the young leaves from the lime tree (also called linden tree) in May. Gather with scissors while the shell-pink scale leaves are still clinging to the opened leaf buds. Cut off the stalks and rinse in water. They can be used in sandwiches, chopped up with a sprinkling of salt and lemon juice, on their own or mixed with chopped up hard-boiled egg. Alternatively mix them with a little cream cheese and use as a spread in sandwiches. See lime flowers on page 119.

GROUND IVY - Glechoma hederacea

This has nothing to do with ivy nor does it look like ivy. Ground ivy is a short creeping plant with heart shaped leaves growing in pairs. Blue flowers grow in clusters and look like violets. The whole plant has a balsamic odour and an aromatic, bitter taste, due to its particular volatile oil, contained in the glands on the under surface of the leaves. It was one of the principal plants used by the early Saxons to clarify their beers, before hops had been introduced, the leaves being steeped in the hot liquor. Hence the names: it was also known as Alehoof and Tunhoof. It not only improved the flavour and keeping qualities of the beer, but made it clearer. Until the reign of Henry VIII it was in general use for this purpose – after that hops were cultivated and used to flavour beer instead. Pick the leaves, dry them and use to make a fragrant tea.

TANSY - Tanacetum vulgare

This plant used to be one of the most commonly grown herbs in cottage gardens and much used medicinally. It was believed that tansy stopped decay and its name derives from the Greek for immortality 'athanatos'. In some ancient cultures its strong antiseptic properties were used to preserve the dead and according to legend a tansy drink was given to Ganymede to make him immortal so that he could be Zeus's cup bearer. At Easter the leaves of this plant were traditionally served with fried eggs and a chopped tansy leaf or two was used to flavour custards, cakes and puddings. The juice used to be extracted from the leaves and used to flavour omelettes – this gave us the tansy omelette. However the leaves have a strong, bitter unpleasant taste with a somewhat lemony aroma. Tansy is a perennial, flowering from July to September and to be seen on roadsides, in hedgerows and waste places. It is an attractive plant with fern-like leaves and clusters of yellow button-shaped flowers. Although associated with Easter in the past, in England the leaves do not really develop until the end of May.

OTHER EDIBLE GREENS include **CAT'S EAR**, a common wild flower with yellow, dandelion like flowers but it is much bigger than a dandelion growing up to 60cm, 2ft tall. Use the leaves in salads. **PENNY-CRESS** is another plant with leaves that have the spicy flavour of watercress – it is a tall plant with tiny white flowers, following by distinctive winged seed pods.

Mushrooms

FAIRY RING MUSHROOMS - Marasmius oreades

This is a common mushroom growing in rings on pastures and lawns from late spring through until late autumn. The ring is easily identifiable because a darker circle of grass is formed known as the 'fairy ring'. These mushrooms tend to be quite small. They work well in soups and stews.

CHICKEN OF THE WOODS - Laetiporus sulphureus

This is a bracket fungus which grows on oak and sweet chestnut as well as yew, cherry and willow from late spring to early autumn but if the winter is mild can be found in early spring. Carefully separate the layers, slice and fry as vegetarian chips. The texture and flavour are like that of chicken.

FAIRY RINGS EN CROUTE
Serves 6 as a starter

6 brown bread rolls
50g, 2oz butter
2 tbsp olive oil
450g, 1lb fairy ring mushrooms, sliced
1 medium onion, peeled and diced
1 clove of garlic, peeled and crushed
4 tbsp Madeira
3 egg yolks, beaten
300ml, ½pt double cream
a little melted butter
50g, 2oz Parmesan cheese, grated

Cut the tops off the bread rolls and scoop out the insides, reserving the bread. Heat the butter and oil in a pan and fry the mushrooms, onion and crushed garlic. Add the Maderia and stir for a minute or two. Mix the egg yolks and cream and add to the mushrooms. Stir over a gentle heat for 10 minutes until the sauce thickens but do not let it boil. Brush melted butter on the insides of the rolls and bake in the oven for 15 minutes to crispen. Spoon the mushroom sauce into the bread roll cavities. Crumble the reserved bread and mix with the Parmesan. Sprinkle on top of the sauce and put under the grill for a couple of minutes to melt the cheese. Serve straightaway.

On the Sea Shore

ROCK SAMPHIRE - Crithmum maritimum

This is a native perennial which is common on the south coast and found on rocks, cliffs and shingle. It flowers from June to August but is best picked in late spring before the flowers appear. To cook rock samphire wash the plant well – this helps get rid of some of the salt – and remove slimy leaves and tough stalks. Boil in water for 10 minutes and serve with melted butter. You may need to separate the fleshy parts from the fibrous veins. You can also use rock samphire in a salad.

ROCK SAMPHIRE PICKLE

450g, 1lb rock samphire leaves
900ml, 1½pts distilled malt vinegar
3 tsp pickling spice
1 tsp ground mace
6 black peppercorns
1 stick of cinnamon

Rinse the samphire and put in a large saucepan with just enough water to cover. Bring to the boil and cook for 8 minutes. Boil the vinegar, water and spices together for 5 minutes and then pour into a bowl and cool. Spoon the samphire into jars, strain the vinegar and fill up the jars so that the samphire is covered with the spiced vinegar. Seal and store for a couple of months to allow the pickle to mellow.

EARLY SUMMER
June

You can still sow beetroot, carrots, French beans, salad leaves and rocket, radishes and turnips. Dig new potatoes and pick broad beans. Broad beans bridge the gap between late spring greens and the main summer crops. You should also be picking salad leaves, radishes and spinach. Later in the month you should be able to pick peas, mangetout and sugar snap peas. Pick edible flowers such as nasturtiums.

In the wild you should be able to gather elderflowers, daisies, clover, bistort, pignuts, sweet cicely, corn and common sow thistle, milk thistle, mallow, burdock and you can still pick cow parsley. On the sea shore you should be able to find dulse, sea beet and marsh and rock samphire. Mushrooms are scarce at this time of year but you might find fairy ring mushrooms and ceps.

It's a busy month because everything grows like mad at this time of year - you will have lots of weeding to do. Try making some elderflower cordial - see recipe on page 83.

CULTIVATED VEGETABLES

POTATOES - Solanum tuberosum

Potatoes originated in the subtropical regions of the Andes in Peru and Chile. Spanish conquistadors conquered Peru in 1536, discovered the potato and brought it back to Spain. Sir John Hawkins is thought to have brought it to Britain in 1563. Sir Francis Drake had potatoes brought to his ship when, during his circumnavigation of the world in 1580, he was anchored off the coast of Peru. The local Indians brought him potatoes and a pig as a gift. Drake brought these back to Britain. Scotland and Ireland were particularly keen of growing potatoes but in 1845 crop failure in Ireland due to blight caused devastating famine. The North Americans probably first experienced the potato from Irish immigrants in the 18th century.

There are many different varieties of potatoes including new potatoes that you can harvest in June. You should obtain seed potatoes in February and chit them by placing in single layers on trays or in egg boxes in a shed. You should place them rose-end up (that is the end with the most eyes from where you can see sprouts starting to form). You should leave the potatoes for about six to eight weeks and they do need light (but not direct sunlight). You should plant tubers in March or early April. Early potatoes are usually ready for lifting when the plants have finished flowering. Potatoes mainly consist of complex carbohydrates in the form of starch but also contain water and protein and are high in Vitamin C and potassium. New potatoes should be cooked and eaten as soon after lifting as possible as the sugars begin to convert to starch straightaway.

HOT POTATO SALAD
Serves 3 – 4

450g, 1lb new potatoes, scrubbed
2 eggs, hard-boiled
2 tbsp olive oil
squeeze of lemon juice
2 tbsp mayonnaise
1 tbsp chives, chopped
1 tbsp parsley, chopped

Cook the potatoes until just tender and drain them. Transfer to a serving dish and while still hot mix in the chopped eggs, olive oil, mayonnaise and lemon juice. Lastly scatter with the parsley and chives. Serve at once.

PEAS AND MANGETOUT - Pisum sativum

Peas are one of the oldest vegetables. Evidence of peas has been found in Burma dated at 9750BC. By the Bronze Age they were used by the peoples of Central Europe and seeds have been found in Switzerland. In these ancient times the peas were dried and formed an important part of the diet because they could be stored and provided protein during winter. The Romans and Greeks were cultivating peas around 500BC and the Romans probably introduced the pea to Britain. At first they were known as pease. It was not until the 18th century that they became peas.

Another type of pea, the edible-podded pea which is harvested when the peas are immature, so that the whole pod is eaten, is called mangetout from the French 'eat-all'. Mangetout is also known in other parts of the world as snow pea, Chinese pea or sugar pea. Then there are asparagus peas which are also known as winged peas – these do not have seeds and are eaten whole with a flavour similar to asparagus. Peas can be sown any time from March through until early June. You could sow at two or three week intervals to give yourself peas over a longer period. Mangetout are particularly nice to grow because they tend to be pricey in the shops – a good variety to try is Carouby de Maussanne which grows like a runner bean plant but has purple flowers and then flat thin pods; Sugar Dwarf Sweet Green and Oregon Sugar Pods are also popular. Sugar snap peas are fun to grow and can be eaten raw in salads as well as lightly cooked. Pick the pods when they are fat but still green and juicy - they are dual purpose - you can leave the pods to grow on a bit and then extract the peas and use the peapods for soup. Peas are a very good source of Vitamin C, A and B and potassium.

PEAPOD SOUP
Serves 3 – 4

This is a very economical soup which actually uses the pods left over after shelling the peas.

1 onion, peeled and sliced
25g, 1oz butter
1 medium potato, peeled and sliced
450g, 1lb peapods
300ml, ½pt milk
300ml, ½pt Marigold Swiss vegetable bouillon stock
salt and pepper
3 tbsp single cream

Gently fry the onion in the butter. Add the potato, peapods, stock and milk. Bring to the boil, cover and simmer until the pods are tender which could take up to 1 hour depending on the size of pods. Liquidise in a blender or food processor and then rub the peapod mixture through a sieve to remove the fibres. Season it, reheat and add a little single cream to each portion if liked.

FRENCH STYLE CREAMY PEAS AND LETTUCE
Serves 4

25g, 1oz butter
6 spring onions, chopped
1 iceberg lettuce
450g, 1lb shelled peas
60ml, 2fl oz Marigold Swiss vegetable bouillon stock
pinch of sugar
salt and pepper
2 tbsp single cream (optional)

Melt the butter in a small casserole and add the spring onions. Cut the iceberg lettuce into quarters and lay on top of the onions. Add the peas, pinch of sugar and seasoning and pour the stock over the vegetables. Cover with a lid and cook gently for about 10 minutes. The liquid should have been absorbed. Stir in the cream if using and serve.

MANGETOUT AND BACON SALAD
Serves 4 – 6

450g, 1lb mangetout or sugar snap peas
100g, 4oz unsmoked bacon, chopped
100g, 4oz Feta cheese, crumbled
50g, 2oz croutons

Dressing
4 tbsp olive oil
½ tbsp lemon juice
½ tbsp white wine vinegar

Trim the ends of the mangetout and blanch in boiling, salted water for a couple of minutes. Arrange in a serving bowl. Dry fry the bacon and scatter over the mangetout along with the crumbled Feta cheese and the croutons. Make the dressing by combining all the ingredients and shaking them together in a screw topped jar. Drizzle the dressing over the salad and serve.

BROAD BEANS - Vicia faba

Broad beans have been around for thousands of years. They are thought to have originated around the Mediterranean, the oldest remains of beans being dated to about 6500BC. Dioscorides described them in his Greek Herbal as 'flatulent, hard of digestion and causing troublesome dreams'. The

Romans introduced them to Britain. They may be the origin of the term 'bean feast'. They were grown in the past by poor people as they are particularly rich in protein and were sustaining during a hard day's work. Broad beans are a useful early summer crop. Plant seeds out in February or March. Try Aquadulce or Red Epicure which produce deep red broad beans. Beware, though, because germination rate is low. Broad beans make attractive plants in the vegetable garden with their black-spotted white flowers which are particularly attractive to bees. However they can be badly affected by black bean aphids. If you pinch off the top of the stem when the pods first begin to form this may help. Planting summer savory alongside the broad bean plants can also discourage black bean aphid. If your plants are clean of aphids, when the first beans at the bottom of the plant start to develop, you can snip off the tops of the shoots and cook them like spinach. Pick pods when the beans begin to show – if picked very young the pods can be eaten whole – leave the pods to become too large and the beans inside will be tough. Broad beans are highly nutritious containing vitamins A and C, an excellent source of phosphorus. They freeze well – wash and blanch in boiling water for 3 minutes.

BROAD BEAN AND MINT SOUP
Serves 3 – 4

1 tbsp sunflower oil
1 onion, peeled and chopped
1 clove of garlic, peeled and crushed
2 potatoes, peeled and sliced
300ml, ½pt Marigold Swiss vegetable bouillon stock
450g, 1lb broad beans
juice of 1 lemon
300ml, ½pt single cream
1 sprig of mint

Heat the oil in a large pan and add the onions and garlic. Cook until softened, then add the potato and stock. Simmer for 20 minutes. Meanwhile cook the broad beans in boiling water for 5 minutes and then add them to the stock and potato. Leave to cool and then add the lemon juice, cream and mint. Purée, reheat and serve.

BROAD BEANS WITH CREAM AND BACON
Serves 6

675g, 1½lb broad beans
a sprig of savory
3 rashers unsmoked streaky bacon, chopped
25g, 1oz butter
3 tbsp double cream
2 tbsp chives

Cook the broad beans in boiling water with the savory added for 5 minutes. Drain and slip the skins off unless the beans are very young. Fry the bacon in a little of the butter and then add the rest along with the beans. Stir in the cream and scatter the chives over the beans just before serving.

CULTIVATED FRUITS

STRAWBERRIES - Fragaria

The strawberry is a symbol of the Virgin Mary. Strawberries were cultivated in this country in Roman times but those that we enjoy today were developed in Virginia, USA and brought back to England by John Tradescant the Elder, the great 17th century gardener. These were crossed with larger yellow Chilean pine strawberries brought over to Europe. It wasn't until the early 1800s that the large modern strawberries were being cultivated and sold in Britain. There are actually two types of strawberries - those that carry a single crop in June and July - popular varieties include Cambridge Favourite, Elsanta and Elvira - and 'perpetual' or remontant varieties that crop slowly in June, reach a peak in August and continue cropping until October - recommended varieties are Mara des Bois and Aromel.

You can also gather wild strawberries (Fragaria vesca) – they tend to grow in open woods and on grassy banks and are smaller versions of the cultivated ones. They have creeping green leaves and small white flowers before the strawberries develop. They have a sharp flavour and go very well with champagne. The Alpine is a wild variety which can also be grown in your garden.

Strawberries are an excellent source of vitamins B and C and contain potassium, iron, fibre and ellagic acid, a phytochemical which may fight against cancer. They are low in calories - 100g of strawberries = 27 calories. If you want a change from strawberries and cream, try them with balsamic vinegar and a little brown sugar or with chopped basil leaves and a little lemon juice. It is well known that freshly ground black pepper will heighten the flavour of strawberries. They should not be washed and do not freeze well.

STRAWBERRY AND LEMON TIPSY TRIFLE
Serves 4 – 6

450g, 1lb strawberries, hulled and quartered
100g, 4oz macaroons
90ml, 3fl oz sweet wine
3 tbsp honey + 2 tbsp brandy
juice of a lemon
150ml, ¼pt double cream
2 egg whites

Mix the strawberries with the biscuits and put in a large glass bowl. Pour 2 tablespoons of the wine over them. Mix together the remaining wine, honey, brandy and 3 tablespoons of lemon juice. Whip the cream and gradually whisk into the wine mixture. Whisk the egg whites and fold into the cream mixture. Pour over the strawberries. Cover and chill for an hour before serving.

STRAWBERRY CREAM ICE
Serves 4 – 6

100g, 4oz granulated sugar + 150ml, ¼pt water
450g, 1lb strawberries, puréed
300ml, ½pt double cream
2 tsp vanilla essence

Dissolve the sugar in the water and simmer until syrupy which will take about 5 minutes. Allow to cool. Mix the strawberry purée with the sugar syrup. Whip the cream until it is thick and then fold into the strawberry mixture. Stir in the vanilla essence and pour the mixture into a freezer container. Freeze for at least 8 hours but remove from the freezer about 30 minutes before you want to serve it.

GARDEN FLOWERS

NASTURTIUM - Tropaeolum majus

Nasturtiums are grown in gardens for their beautiful flowers but the plant is also valuable as a herb. Seeds should be planted in late spring in full sun – the plants grow quickly and will climb if support is provided or hang over a wall. Be warned though you may find black aphids a problem. Nasturtiums will flower in late June and go on flowering until the first frosts. You can use the leaves and flowers in salads – they have a strong peppery taste, not unlike watercress. Lots of seeds will be scattered on the ground by the end of summer - pickle these as a substitute for capers, use in salads or grind up and use like pepper. In folklore a lotion made from leaves, flowers and seeds mixed with nettles and 3 oak leaves was said to prevent baldness.

IN THE WILD
Wild Flowers and Greens

ELDERFLOWERS (Elder = sambucus nigra)

The elder is native to Britain, Europe and Scandinavia. It is thought the Romans may have imported the elder to Britain. The plant has been highly valued for centuries. The wood was used in the past for making musical instruments. The elder was regarded in the past as a sacred tree and people believed they would be cursed if they cut down or destroyed an elder. This old belief originated from the apostle Judas who was said to have hanged himself on a cross made from an elder tree. Those who gather firewood will avoid elder for burning, not because it burns badly but because to burn it is to 'raise the devil.' Widespread in hedgerows, woods and on roadside verges the elder is a tall, fast growing shrub which has a dual purpose. The elderflowers appear in June and the berries in September. Elderflowers make a great cordial and work well with gooseberries and strawberries.

ELDERFLOWER FRITTERS
Makes 10 fritters

100g, 4oz plain flour
2 small eggs
300ml, ½pt milk
10 small elderflower heads
sunflower oil for deep frying

Make up the batter by beating together the flour, eggs and milk. Wash and trim the elderflower heads leaving a stalk and dip them in the batter. Heat the oil in a frying pan and fry the fritters using the stalk to remove each one when it is golden brown. Trim off the stalks and serve with caster sugar and lemon juice.

ELDERFLOWER CORDIAL

This is a great drink to make in June when elderflowers are in season.

2 large lemons, sliced
25 elderflower heads
50g, 2oz citric acid (can be bought at the chemist)
1. 3litre, 2½pts water
1.6kg, 3½lb granulated sugar
¼ Campden tablet

Place the water and granulated sugar in a large saucepan and bring to the boil gradually to dissolve the sugar. Remove from the heat. Place the elderflowers, slices of lemon, and citric acid in a large plastic container and pour over the sugar syrup. Cover with a lid or cloth and leave to infuse for up to 5 days, stirring every day. Strain through muslin. If you want the cordial to keep for longer than a couple of weeks, add ¼ Campden tablet dissolved in a tablespoon of water to the strained syrup. Pour into sterilised bottles and store or freeze in suitable containers.

ELDERFLOWER CHAMPAGNE

4 litres, 8pts water
750g, 1½lb granulated sugar
5 large elderflower heads
1 lemon and 1 orange, sliced
2 tbsp white wine vinegar

Boil the water and pour it over the sugar. When it is cold, add the elderflowers, the sliced lemon and orange and the vinegar. Cover with a thick cloth and leave for 24 hours. Squeeze the flowers and strain through muslin. Store in large containers and leave for 10 days, by which time the natural yeast should have produced a sparkling drink.

CLOVER - **Trifolium pratense**
DAISY - **Bellis perennis**

Clover and daisies can be found everywhere during the summer and I wonder if you realise that both are edible. Red and white clovers are the most common types and are recognised by their trefoil leaves. You can make clover tea by pouring boiling water over a handful of flowers and leaves. You can also make clover wine – make in the same way as coltsfoot wine (see page 27). Clover is cultivated in this country for animal feed – its value as fodder for cattle gives us the phrase 'Live or Be in Clover'. It is said that 'when you can put your foot on seven daisies, summer has come'. Both the leaves and flowers of clover and daisies can be added to salads; clover leaves can be cooked in the same way as spinach.

BISTORT **Also known as Snakeweed**
Polygonum bistorta

This plant has distorted underground stems so the botanical name is appropriately 'bistorta' from the Latin 'bis' meaning twice and 'tortus' meaning twisted. Bistort grows about 60cm, 2ft high with pink flowery spikes on top of straight hairless stems. The leaves are triangular or arrow-shaped. You can find it in wet, hilly pastures but only in the North of the country. It flowers from June to August. The plant is featured in the Great Unicorn Tapestries in the Cloisters in New York with its pink flower touching the foreleg of the white unicorn. Bistort leaves can be used raw in salads or added to soups.

In the Lake District the leaves are an important ingredient of Easter Ledge Pudding for which there are many variations. Traditionally it should be eaten during the last two weeks of Lent by ladies who are hoping to become mothers. It is also nicknamed 'best birth pudding'. Here is a recipe from *'Good Things in England'* by Florence White.

EASTER LEDGE PUDDING

Several handfuls of edible young green herbs or weeds such
as young nettle tops, dandelion leaves, bistort, washed
1 hard boiled egg
1 raw egg, beaten
15g, ½oz butter

Boil the greens in water for 10 minutes. Strain and chop up the leaves. Add the boiled egg, chopped up small. Add the raw egg, butter and a little salt and pepper. Mix together, heat through and then turn into a pudding basin and leave to cool. Turn out and serve with meat.

PIGNUTS Also known as Earthnuts - Conopodium majus

Once upon a time children used to dig up pignuts, a favourite wayside nibble. The nuts can be eaten raw, once they have been scraped and washed. The plant is an umbellifer, a relation to parsley, and can be found in open woodland and on the edges of woods, hedgerows, meadows and sandy heaths in June and July. The plant lives for a number of years having an underground part from which the annual stems sprout each spring, dying down again in the autumn. Years ago, pigs were turned loose in the woods to search for acorns and other food.

By rooting and nuzzling with their snouts, the pigs found the knobbly underground portion of the plant – farmers were aware how much the pigs liked these 'nuts' from the ground and pignut was deemed an appropriate name. The plant is delicate and small with tiny white flowers and the leaves are feathery, like dill. The root is the important part but you cannot just pull up the plant with the root attached, because the leaf stalk will break. You must dig into the ground with a trowel to obtain the edible root. The root size will vary but usually has a diameter of about 2.5cm, 1in. The taste is like that of a chestnut. You can eat them raw or simmer for a few minutes in salted water.

SWEET CICELY - Myrrhis odorata

Sweet cicely is a wild herb also known as myrrh. It looks very similar to cow parsley but is larger with white umbels of flowers on long stalks. The leaves often have small white flecks on them. They are a valuable sweetener and in this case 'sweet' in the name really means sweet. The feathery fern-like leaves have a mild aniseed flavour and are suitable for flavouring stewed fruits. Some people say that you can halve the amount of sugar usually used in jellies and jams by adding sweet cicely. Unfortunately it is not a common plant and more often found on grassy roadsides in the North and Scotland. It is possible to cultivate sweet cicely in your garden. You can pick the leaves at any time. You can also use the unripe seeds. Apparently crushed seeds used to be used as furniture polish. You can add the seeds to fruit salads or add to cooked dishes such as apple pie. Leaves can be added to salads, especially if you are using bitter leaves such as sorrel or dandelion. The roots can also be cooked as for a root vegetable such as parsnip. The plant produces white flowers in May and June.

CORN SOW THISTLE - Sonchus arvensis

Theseus is said to have dined off a dish of sow thistles before conquering the Minotaur. The corn sow thistle is a perennial, tall plant with yellow, thistle-like leaves and flowers. You can eat the leaves in a salad but first you have to trim off the bristles from the edges. You can also cook the leaves in a little water, as you would spinach.

COMMON or SMOOTH SOW THISTLE
Sonchus oleraceus

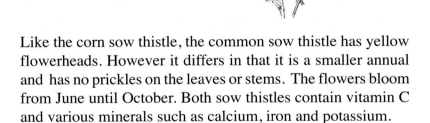

Like the corn sow thistle, the common sow thistle has yellow flowerheads. However it differs in that it is a smaller annual and has no prickles on the leaves or stems. The flowers bloom from June until October. Both sow thistles contain vitamin C and various minerals such as calcium, iron and potassium.

MILK THISTLE - Silybum marianum

The milk thistle has purple flowers, which appear between June and September and the leaves are shiny dark green with white veins and spiny edges. Milk thistles, also known as Silybum, commonly grow near the sea and can be up to 1.8m, 6ft tall. These thistles are useful for the stems, which can be peeled and stewed like rhubarb or steamed and eaten like asparagus.

It is advisable to soak the stems in water first to remove some of the bitterness. The spiny bracts that surround the flowerheads can also be eaten like globe artichokes. The seeds are very useful and are used in alternative medicine. In fact milk thistle has been used for thousands of years as a remedy for a variety of ailments, especially liver problems. Dioscorides recommended the seeds as a bitter tonic, capable of powerfully rejuvenating the liver, and Arabian physicians used the plant both to stimulate the appetite and the digestive processes, to promote bile, to strengthen liver function and to treat poisoning, jaundice and help treat hepatitis. Silymarin, which can be extracted from the seeds, is believed to be the biologically active part of the plant. If you can gather enough seeds you could try making your own tincture (these are alcohol based usually with 10% herb and 90% alcohol). Fill a jar a third full with milk thistle seeds. Use 100% proof vodka to fill up the jar. Seal and shake daily for a week; then leave for another four weeks. Take a few drops at a time – no more than 1ml. Otherwise you can buy milk thistle capsules in health food shops.

LESSER BURDOCK Also known as Pig's Rhubarb
Arctium minus

This is a biennial plant found throughout Britain on roadside verges, edges of woods and waste places. It has huge heart-shaped leaves which drape themselves over the ground. You can pick the young leaf stems, peel off the outer part, cut into short lengths and use them raw in salads or boil and serve like asparagus. Flowering from July to September, flowerheads are egg-shaped and thistle-like, turning into prickly burrs. You can also dig up the roots and boil as a vegetable (popular in Japan) or use to make dandelion and burdock beer (see Dandelion beer on page 32 - use half burdock and half dandelion roots).

COMMON MALLOW - **Malva sylvestris**

Mallow is a perennial or sometimes biennial which flowers from June to September - it has large pale mauve flowers with purple veins and five petals. It has large crinkly leaves which near the root have a dark purple blotch at the centre. Mallow is found on rough ground and roadside verges mostly in the South and often near the sea. Pick the mallow leaves in June when they are pale green and tender. They will have quite a rubbery texture. Use them as soon as possible. The seeds which appear later in the year are also edible – they have a triangular shape and used to be called cheeses and eaten by children in the country. Mallow leaves are glutinous and therefore useful as a natural thickener in soups. In Egypt the leaves of a very similar species are the basis of the soup, melokhia, a national dish.

DEEP FRIED MALLOW
Deep fry in sunflower or rape seed oil until crisp.

MALLOW SOUP
Serves 2 – 3

2 tbsp olive oil
2 onions, peeled and chopped
1 medium potato, peeled and sliced
2 cloves of garlic, peeled and crushed
½ tsp of ground coriander
600ml, 1pt Marigold Swiss vegetable bouillon stock
2 handfuls of mallow leaves
3 tbsp single cream

Heat the oil in a saucepan and sauté the onions and potato. Add the garlic and coriander. Then add the stock and bring to the boil. Simmer for 10 minutes. Add the leaves. Simmer for another 10 minutes and then put in the blender and liquidise. Serve each portion with a little cream.

Mushrooms

CEPS
Also known as Penny Bun or Porcini - Boletus edulis

Gather ceps from June until October. There are two types: boletus edulis and boletus aereus which is known as a summer cep. Ceps can be found in the undergrowth in spruce forests or in beech woods but usually in acid soils. They are big and instead of gills have a layer of vertical tubes, looking like a sponge. In a fresh specimen the pores will appear white, but if too old they will be yellowish. Ceps are a warm chestnut brown and have a pungent, nutty flavour.

Drying CEPS
Cut away any soggy parts – you may have to cut away the tubes (the parts underneath which look like a sponge, if they are wet). Cut the caps into 5cm, 2in pieces. Thread the pieces of mushroom on a string using a darning needle and hang them in a warm dry place such as an airing cupboard until dried and brittle. To reconstitute, soak in boiling water for an hour. They will actually have a richer flavour than they would have had if eaten fresh.

CEP FILLED PUFF PASTRY TARTS
Serves 4

175g, 6oz puff pastry
25g, 1oz butter
175g, 6oz ceps, sliced
2 tbsp soured cream
juice of ½ a lemon
sprinkling of black pepper

Roll out the pastry and line 4 tartlet tins. Bake blind for 15 minutes until puffed and golden. Melt the butter in a frying pan and sauté the ceps, stirring them in the butter for a couple of minutes. Add the soured cream, lemon juice and pepper. Fill the tartlets with the mushroom mixture and serve.

On the Sea Shore

DULSE - Rhodymenia palmata

Dulse is a seaweed growing all round the coasts of Britain. You can gather it in June when it is young and at its best. You will find the red-brown fan-like fronds attached to rocks just below the tide line. Cut off the fronds with scissors, leaving the stem so that it can grow again. Dulse is rich in potassium and magnesium and tastes a bit like oysters. It is tough so it is best to soak it in cold water for a couple of hours before using. Then you can cut it into pieces and eat it raw. To cook dulse you need to simmer it in water or milk for a couple of hours. You could then mix it with mashed potato and parsley and some more milk and serve it with meat or fish. To dry dulse wash it well and lay an old piece of material outside – obviously choose a dry, sunny day! Spread the dulse out on it and leave until dry and crisp – it will shrink as it dries. Store in glass jars or brown paper bags. To reconstitute soak in cold water for 10 minutes.

STIR FRIED DULSE

Olive oil for frying
1 onion, peeled and sliced
50g, 2oz dried dulse
1 tbsp soya sauce

Heat the oil in a wok and fry the onion on a high heat, then add the dulse and toss around for 2 minutes until it darkens and softens. Add the soya sauce and sesame seeds, stir and serve at once.

MARSH SAMPHIRE Also known as Glasswort
Salicornia herbacea

Marsh samphire grows all round the coasts of Britain but grows most prolifically on the South, East and West coasts of England. It is an annual and grows commonly on sandy mud in salt marshes and the best samphire is that found just below the tide line. So you need to go out at low tide wearing wellies. Beware, you may get covered in mud picking your samphire but it will be worth it. Traditionally it is best picked on the longest day of the year! It looks like a cactus with its branchlike stems. The flowers are also green and so not very noticeable. Samphire is rich in soda and used to be used for making glass, hence the name glasswort. It is at its best when young, about 10cm, 4in high, bright green and before it gets a string growing through the centre of the stem. It is best if you cut the stems off with scissors. You can eat it once the stringy bit has developed and just strip the green flesh off with a fork or with your teeth. In this case pick the whole plant in July and August and cook and serve it like asparagus. It is delicious in a salad or cooked as a green vegetable to serve with fish. Wash the samphire in cold water before cooking – you can store it unwashed in a plastic bag in the fridge for two or three days. Be warned that samphire can taste very salty.

PICKLED SAMPHIRE

Use young shoots of samphire, cut into 2.5cm, 1in lengths, pack into jars and cover with spiced vinegar. Use distilled malt vinegar – to one litre, 2 pints add 2 tablespoons of cloves, allspice berries, small piece of root ginger, one stick of cinnamon and one tablespoon of white peppercorns. Transfer to a saucepan and heat gently. Cover and leave on the lowest heat for 2 hours. Cool and strain.

MARSH SAMPHIRE MAYONNAISE

50g, 2oz marsh samphire
2 egg yolks
1 tsp mustard powder
120ml, 4fl oz olive oil
120ml, 4fl oz sunflower oil
3 tbsp white wine vinegar

Blanch the samphire for a minute in boiling water and then drain and run cold water over it. Put the egg yolk in a food processor or a bowl, mix in the mustard powder and then add the oil drip by drip beating or processing as you go. Halfway through add the vinegar and then continue to add the oil drip by drip until the mayonnaise is thick and creamy. Fold in the samphire.

CREAMY MARSH SAMPHIRE
Serves 4

225g, 8oz young marsh samphire
150ml, ¼pt double cream
3 tbsp fresh parsley
seasoning of pepper

Blanch the samphire as in the previous recipe. Heat the cream until just below boiling point, add the samphire and parsley and season with pepper. Cover and simmer for 2 minutes. Serve immediately as a vegetable accompaniment.

MID TO LATE SUMMER
July and August

Plant final crops of beetroot, kale, radicchio and endive, oriental greens such as mizuna, mustard spinach, pak choi, carrots and radishes. Vegetables that you could be picking include lettuce, French and runner beans which come into their own now. Early beetroot should be ready and you should still have mangetout, rocket, spinach and some carrots and potatoes to dig up. Gather edible flowers such as lavender, nasturtium leaves and rose petals from your garden. There are plenty of fruits now ripening. Apart from strawberries the following fruits are now at their best: raspberries, redcurrants, blackcurrants, blueberries and cherries. In August mulberries and early plums will be ready.

From the wild you can gather blackberries, crab apples, meadowsweet, lime flowers, and rest-harrow. Possible mushrooms to hunt for are parasols, chanterelles, giant puffballs and hedgehog fungus. From the sea shore you should be able to bring home sea beet, rock samphire, sea blite and sea purslane.

Last year I grew asparagus peas – low spreading plants produce pretty red flowers which then become asparagus peas. These should be picked and eaten when they are about 4cm, 1½in long. Leave them until they are longer and they will be stringy. They are delicious cooked in boiling, salted water for about 6 minutes. I found steaming didn't work so well.

CULTIVATED VEGETABLES

LETTUCE - Lactuca sativa

Lettuce has a long and fascinating history dating back to 6000BC in Egypt where there is evidence on wall paintings that the Egyptians ate lettuce. Darius, King of Persia, certainly served lettuce around 500BC. The Greeks and Romans cultivated a cos-type lettuce. The Cos lettuce derives its name from the island of Cos. The word lactuca comes from the Latin and refers to the milky, lactic sap that you can see when you cut a lettuce. The Romans believed this sap had medicinal properties. It is in fact highly narcotic and can be used as a substitute for opium. The Greeks valued lettuces because of their soporific effect. The Romans are thought to have introduced lettuce to Britain. There are four types of lettuce, Butterhead, Loose Leaf, Cos and Crisphead (Iceberg being the most common). The Loose Leaf are the type that do not form hearts and there are now many varieties of these which are also known as 'cut and come again' - pick a few leaves from each plant and new ones form in their place. Butterhead types form a heart but the leaves are soft and delicate. The Cos lettuce forms an upright, elongated heart and takes longer to mature than other types. The Crisphead, of which the Iceberg and Webb's Wonderful are varieties, takes on the appearance of a cabbage with succulent, crisp and wrinkled leaves.

There are so many varieties of lettuce available now that if you plant carefully you can have different types of lettuce growing in your garden all year round. Start planting seeds under cloches in February and you should be eating salad leaves in May. Continue to sow seeds all through the summer and plant autumn varieties such as Winter Density which will survive the winter without protection. There are many different coloured lettuces you can grow from pale to dark green to green speckled with red to red-tinted to almost completely crimson. Red Salad Bowl, Lollo Rossa and Marvel of Four Seasons are all easy and fun to grow and are cut and come again lettuces. The greener the leaves, as a rule, the more nutritious the lettuce, providing more beta carotene. Lettuces are a good source of folate. They contain 95% water.

Lesser Celandine (see page 16)

Alexanders
(see page 36)

Alexanders Stem

Hairy Bittercress (see page 18)

Coltsfoot Flowers (see page 26)

Wood Sorrel (see page 42)

Hogweed Shoots (see page 45)

Wild Garlic
(see page 29)

Red Valerian
(see page 65)

St George's Mushroom
(see page 49)

Good King Henry
(see page 38)

Chicken of
the Woods
(see page 70)

Asparagus Peas
(see page 95)

Variegated Lemon Balm (see page 48)

Goosegrass
(see page 214)

Mallow
(see page 90)

Sloes
(see page 182)

Common
Puffballs
(see page
126)

Silverweed
(see page 202)

Jew's Ear
Mushrooms
(see page 19)

Chickweed
(see page 215)

Yarrow in Flower
(see page 217)

CAESAR SALAD
Serves 6

2 Cos lettuces
6 anchovy fillets
2 cloves of garlic, peeled and crushed
½ tsp English mustard
few drops of Worcestershire sauce
150ml, ¼pt olive oil
2 egg yolks
juice of 1 lemon
50g, 2oz Parmesan cheese
50g, 2oz croutons

Chop the Cos into bite-sized pieces. Put the anchovies, garlic, mustard and Worcestershire sauce in a large bowl and add a few croutons. Mash the ingredients to a thick, smooth paste. Add lemon juice and egg yolks and stir together. Add half the Parmesan and pour the oil in a thin stream beating the dressing as you go. Toss in the lettuce and the rest of the croutons.

RUNNER AND FRENCH BEANS
Phaseolus coccineus and Phaseolus vulgaris

It is thought that French beans originated in Peru around 8000BC and from there the vegetable spread throughout South and Central America. They were introduced to Europe in the 16th century by Spanish explorers returning from their voyages to the New World. They were first called kidney beans, alluding to the shape of the seeds. They became known as French beans because they were imported from France. In the early days only the seeds were eaten and they were known as flageolets or dried as haricots. Runner beans are similar to French Beans, the difference being they have larger, coarser and stronger flavoured pods. Runner beans originated in Mexico around

1000BC and when first introduced to Britain in the 1600s were used only as ornamental climbers. It wasn't until the 18th century that the British realised the pods were edible. The variety that seems most popular is Scarlet Emperor which has, as the name suggests, scarlet flowers.

Recommended climbing varieties of French beans are Blue Lake, yellow-podded Meraviglia di Venezia and purple-podded Cosse Violette. I have grown the Meraviglia di Venezia which crop very heavily but later on in October – the danger is that the plants can be ruined by frost before you have finished harvesting the beans. Dwarf varieties can also be grown. None of these varieties should be sown until the danger of frost is past, at the end of May. Good dwarf French bean varieties are Purple Queen, Sungold and Mont d'Or (yellow-podded) and Tendergreen which is a traditional stringless green-podded variety. Green beans are an excellent source of vitamins K, A and C and potassium. They are also a good source of fibre.

RUNNER BEANS WITH MUSHROOM SAUCE
Serves 4

450g, 1lb runner beans, topped, tailed and sliced
50g, 2oz butter
1 onion, peeled and chopped
100g, 4oz mushrooms, sliced
squeeze of lemon juice
6 tbsp single cream

Cook the beans in boiling water until just tender and drain them. Melt the butter in a frying pan and fry the onion gently until soft. Add the mushrooms and squeeze a little lemon juice over them. Cook for 5 minutes. Add the beans and stir in the cream. Simmer over a low heat for 3 minutes by which time the sauce should have thickened. Serve as a side dish.

RUNNER BEANS AU GRATIN
Serves 4

450g, 1lb runner beans
15g, ½oz butter
1 red onion, peeled and sliced
1 tbsp plain flour
300ml, ½pt milk
2 tbsp brown breadcrumbs
50g, 2oz mature Cheddar cheese, grated

Cook the runner beans in boiling salted water for a few minutes. Melt the butter in a small saucepan and add the onion. Cook until softened, then stir in the flour and gradually add the milk stirring until you have a smooth sauce. Transfer the runner beans to an ovenproof dish and pour the onion sauce over them. Sprinkle with the breadcrumbs and cheese and cook in the oven for 20 minutes at gas mark 4, 180°C (350°F) until golden and bubbling on top.

SAUTÉED FRENCH BEANS WITH RED PEPPER
Serves 3 – 4

450g, 1lb French beans, topped and tailed
2 tbsp olive oil + 15g, ½oz butter
1 red pepper, deseeded and sliced
2 spring onions, sliced
1 tbsp pine nuts, roasted

Bring a pan of water to the boil and add the beans. Cook them for 3 or 4 minutes and then drain and refresh under cold water. Heat the oil and butter in a large frying pan and add the red pepper. Cook for a couple of minutes and then add the French beans and spring onions. Sauté for a few minutes. Sprinkle with pine nuts and serve.

GARDEN FLOWERS

There may be several flowers and herbs growing in your garden with edible petals. Borage flowers are a lively bright blue and are traditionally added to Pimms. You can also decorate salads with them. Pot marigolds (calendula) are useful as the petals can be used instead of saffron to impart a yellow colour to rice dishes. The Romans used marigold as an alternative to saffron and brought the flower to Britain. You can dry the marigold petals and keep them in an airtight container – they are aromatic and slightly bitter. Marigold petals added to melted butter and stirred into some boiled new potatoes add a new flavour.

Have you ever used chive flowers or do you usually pick them off the tops of your chives and discard them? They are such a lovely violet colour – try adding some to a coleslaw of carrot and white cabbage. Alternatively add them to salads – they add a mild onion flavour. You could also try a chive vinegar – steep a handful of chive flowers in white vinegar and leave for 2 weeks – strain off the flowers – you will be left with a beautiful pink vinegar which has a mild oniony flavour.

The petals of roses, pansies, violets, violas, pinks (also known as carnations, gillyflowers, alpine or border pinks) are all edible and add colour to salads. They can also be used to decorate cakes and puddings. Even sweet peas are edible – you can toss the flowers into vinaigrette or infuse them in sugar or syrup. Try adding honeysuckle when you make an apple jelly. Lilies can be used – Americans fry them in batter and in France they are steeped in honey. The buds can also be pickled. Other edible flowers include Sweet Williams, lilacs, cornflowers, gladiolas, freesias and fuchsias. Also edible are many of the herb flowers such as marjoram, thyme, hyssop and dill.

Lavender produces lovely blue flowers in July which can be dried. The Romans used lavender and in fact the Latin name 'lavandula' comes from 'lavare' meaning to wash. Romans bathed with lavender and used it to heal wounds. You can add fresh or dried lavender to biscuit recipes – less aromatic when cooked – it adds a gingery flavour.

GIN AND LAVENDER ICE CREAM
Serves 4

5 tbsp gin
1 tbsp dried lavender flowers
5 egg yolks, warmed
175g, 6oz clear honey
300ml, ½pt double cream

Warm the gin a little and pour over the lavender. Leave to infuse for an hour. Strain through a sieve extracting as much gin from the lavender as possible. Beat the egg yolks until thick and creamy, add the honey gradually while continuing to whisk. Stir in the flavoured gin. Whip the cream and fold it in. Transfer to a freezer container and freeze until firm.

LAVENDER SHORTBREAD
Makes 8 pieces

100g, 4oz butter
50g, 2oz caster sugar
175g, 6oz plain flour
1 tsp dried lavender flowers
few drops lavender essence or syrup
finely grated rind from ½ a lemon

Cream together the butter and caster sugar, work in the flour and then stir in the lavender flowers, essence and grated lemon. Press into a greased round 20cm, 8in tin and bake in the oven at gas mark 4, 180°C (350°F) for 20 minutes. Cut into triangles.

LAVENDER VINEGAR

8 sprigs dried lavender
450ml, ¾pt white wine vinegar

Put the lavender into a bottle with the vinegar and leave on a sunny window-sill for a couple of weeks – you can then use it to flavour salad dressings.

LEMON GERANIUM is a great plant to grow in a pot – it will need to come inside for the winter months. The leaves make a wonderful sorbet as do rose petals.

LEMON GERANIUM SORBET
Serves 4 - 6

75g, 3oz granulated sugar
4 lemon geranium leaves
juice of 1 lemon
1 egg white

Dissolve the sugar in 300ml, ½pt of water and boil for 2 or 3 minutes. Take off the heat and add the geranium leaves. Cover and leave to infuse for 30 minutes. Stir in the lemon juice and strain into a freezer container. When completely cold freeze until slushy. Beat the egg white and fold it into the slushy mixture. Return to the freezer and freeze until firm.

ROSE PETAL SORBET
Serves 6 - 8

600ml, 1pt water
225g, 8oz granulated sugar
handful of scented rose petals, yellow ends removed
1 strip pared lemon rind
juice of 1 small lemon
2 egg whites

Put the water and sugar in a saucepan and bring slowly to the boil, stirring until the sugar dissolves. Add the petals and lemon rind. Boil for 10 minutes and then leave to cool. Strain the syrup, pressing the petals to extract all the juice. Add the lemon juice and pour into a container. Freeze until the slushy stage, then beat the mixture to break down ice crystals. Whisk the egg whites and fold them into the sorbet. Return to the freezer and freeze until firm.

CULTIVATED FRUITS

REDCURRANTS - Ribes sativum

Redcurrants are native European fruits, grown in gardens in Britain from the 1500s. Although closely related to blackcurrants and often combined with them in summer puddings (see page 107) they are quite different. Plants are pruned and cared for like gooseberries and grow on old wood. The bushes are long-lived and can tolerate poor soil conditions.

They have a soft skin and can be eaten raw when very ripe. Whitecurrants are similar to redcurrants but lack the pigment. Like blackcurrants, redcurrants are also a good source of Vitamin C but are also high in potassium.

REDCURRANT JELLY
Makes about 1.5kg, 3lb

Redcurrants are naturally rich in pectin and acid so do not need a preserving sugar. Being acidic they need a high proportion of sugar.

1kg, 2.2lb redcurrants
900ml, 1½pts water
675g, 1½lb granulated sugar

Put the redcurrants in a saucepan with the water and heat slowly. Simmer until the redcurrants are soft. Mash them with a wooden spoon and strain through muslin. Put the juice in a large saucepan with the sugar. Heat gently, stirring until the sugar has dissolved, then boil rapidly until setting point is reached. Pour into small jars and seal.

REDCURRANT SORBET
Serves 4 - 6

You can also make this sorbet with half redcurrants and half raspberries.

450g, 1lb redcurrants
225g, 8oz sugar
juice of 1 small lemon
1 egg white

To make the sorbet heat the redcurrants in a little water until the juices run. Sieve to remove the pips and make up to 600ml, 1pt with a little water if necessary. Heat the redcurrant juice with the sugar until dissolved and then simmer for 5 minutes. Leave to cool, covering with a lid to stop a skin forming. Transfer to a freezer container and freeze until slushy. Beat with a whisk. Beat the egg white and gently fold it in. Return to the freezer and freeze until firm.

CUMBERLAND SAUCE

A spicy sauce for serving with pork, poultry or game.

100g, 4oz redcurrants
50g, 2oz sugar
1 shallot, peeled and finely chopped
juice and grated rind of ½ an orange and ½ a lemon
150ml, ¼pt port
½ tsp mustard powder
¼ tsp ground ginger

Put the redcurrants in a saucepan with 150ml, ¼pt of water and cook to soften the fruit. Sieve the redcurrants and stir the sugar into the redcurrant juice. Cook until syrupy, add the shallot, orange and lemon juice and rind, the port, mustard and ginger. Mix together and serve hot or cold.

BLACKCURRANTS - Ribes nigrum

Blackcurrants grow wild all over Europe. The English started to cultivate them in the 1600s. They are very rich in vitamin C and contain the antioxidant, carotenoid lutein. They are high in pectin and therefore suitable for jams and jellies. Blackcurrants are too acidic to eat on their own but are wonderful cooked with sugar, puréed and added to yoghurt or other fruits. They are easy to grow and you can expect each bush to produce a good yield of fruit in the summer. They freeze very well.

BLACKCURRANT SPONGE PUDDING
Serves 6 - 8

225g, 8oz blackcurrants
50g, 2oz granulated sugar
100g, 4oz self-raising flour
1 tsp baking powder
2 eggs
100g, 4oz caster sugar
100g, 4oz butter

Spread the blackcurrants and sugar over the base of a greased ovenproof dish. Put the flour, baking powder, eggs, sugar and butter in a food processor and process until you have a smooth mixture. Spread over the top of the blackcurrants and cook in the oven at gas mark 4, 180°C (350°F) for 35 – 40 minutes. Serve hot with cream or ice cream.

BLACKCURRANT KISSEL
Serves 4 - 6

This pudding is quite runny and has the consistency of thick soup. It goes well with a lemon or vanilla ice cream.

450g, 1lb blackcurrants
3 tbsp clear honey
juice of 1 lemon
pinch of nutmeg
1 – 2 tbsp caster sugar
25g, 1oz wholemeal flour

Put the blackcurrants, honey and lemon juice into a saucepan with enough cold water just to cover the fruit. Heat gently and simmer until the fruit is soft. Sieve the fruit and add a pinch of nutmeg. At this stage taste the purée. If it is too tart add one or two tablespoons of caster sugar. Put the flour into a bowl and stir in some of the blackcurrant mixture to make a paste. Mix this paste into the rest of the purée and stir over a low heat until thickened. Cool before serving.

SUMMER PUDDING
Serves 6

900g, 2lb mixed blackcurrants, redcurrants, raspberries
175g, 6oz caster sugar
8 – 10 slices wholemeal bread, crusts removed

Cook the black and redcurrants adding 2 tablespoons of water and the sugar. After a few minutes add the raspberries and cook for a couple more minutes. Use the slices of bread to line a 1 litre, 2 pint basin including the bottom. Pour the cooked fruit into the bowl with all the juices. Press a slice of bread down on top and cover with a plate and a weight. Refrigerate overnight. When ready to serve, run a knife around the sides and turn the pudding out.

RASPBERRIES - Rubus idaeas

Wild raspberries have been around since prehistoric times but were not cultivated until the Middle Ages. Today you can still find wild raspberries which do have thorns, although they are much smaller than cultivated ones. They grow mainly in wooded areas. They are a good source of Vitamin C and potassium and they are one of the best fresh fruit sources of fibre. Raspberries contain an important antioxidant, ellagic acid. They are low in calories – 100g = 25 calories. They are more versatile than strawberries and freeze very well. If you have some room and want to grow some summer/autumn fruits then I highly recommend raspberries and in particular Autumn Bliss. If you plant a few canes these will multiply each year (rather like mint which spreads its roots). You will end up with a really good supply of raspberries – the canes start cropping in August and go on through September. I have a freezer packed with raspberries. It is also well worth having a couple of redcurrant bushes. Raspberries and redcurrants go really well together in a sorbet or ice cream.

RASPBERRY TIRAMISU
Serves 4

350g, 12oz raspberries
half a packet of sponge fingers
60ml, 2fl oz framboise
225g, 8oz mascarpone
2 eggs
50g, 2oz icing sugar
1 tbsp brandy

Lay the sponge fingers in layers in a round bowl. Pour over the framboise and scatter raspberries on top. Beat the egg yolks into the mascarpone with the icing sugar and tablespoon of brandy. Whisk the egg whites separately and fold them in. Spoon over the raspberries. Chill before serving.

RASPBERRY AND REDCURRANT JAM
Makes about 2.5kg, 5lb

To every 450g, 1lb raspberries use:
450g, 1lb granulated sugar
150ml, ¼pt redcurrant juice (redcurrants cooked with some
water and sieved)

Gently crush the raspberries and transfer to a large saucepan. Bring to the boil slowly, and then boil for 15 minutes. Add the sugar and redcurrant juice and when the sugar has dissolved boil until setting point is reached. Skim any scum off the surface. Cool slightly, pot and cover.

RASPBERRY VINEGAR
Makes about 1.7 litres, 3 pints

675g, 1½lb raspberries
1 litre, 2pts distilled white malt vinegar
1kg, 2.2lb granulated sugar

Put the raspberries, with water to cover, in a large saucepan and simmer for 30 minutes, partially covered. Strain off the juice and put into a pan with the vinegar and sugar. Stir to dissolve the sugar over a gentle heat. Bring to the boil and simmer for 10 minutes until the liquid becomes syrupy. Pour into sterilised bottles and cork.

LOGANBERRIES, TAYBERRIES, BOYSENBERRIES - Rubus Hybrids

Loganberries are a hybrid from the American dewberry and raspberry. Boysenberries are another variation and are thought to be a cross between blackberry, loganberry and raspberry. Tayberries are a cross between a blackberry and raspberry. They were first cultivated in Scotland where raspberries were crossed with American blackberries. Dr Derek Jennings bred the first tayberries at the Scottish Crop Research Institute and the tayberry is named after the river Tay. They are thought to be the most successful hybrid berry. All these berries can be bought as cultivated plants and grown in your garden.

TAYBERRY AND CHOCOLATE TARTLETS
Makes 4 – 5 tartlets

For the pastry
225g, 8oz plain flour
125g, 5oz butter
3 tbsp icing sugar
1 egg yolk

Topping

100g, 4oz milk chocolate
225g, 8oz fromage frais
175g, 6oz Greek yoghurt
350g, 12oz tayberries
icing sugar

Put all the ingredients for the pastry into a food processor and process until the mixture binds together. Wrap in cling film and chill for 30 minutes. Then roll out into rounds and fit into the base of four or five greased tartlet tins. Prick and bake blind in the oven at gas mark 4, 180°C (350°F) for 10 to 15 minutes and allow to cool. Divide the tayberries between the tartlets. To make the topping beat together the fromage frais and yoghurt. Melt the chocolate and quickly stir into the fromage frais mixture. It will start setting immediately. Spoon over the tayberries. Dust with icing sugar and serve.

LOGANBERRY SNOW CREAM
Serves 4

350g, 12oz loganberries
1 tbsp rosewater
50g, 2oz caster sugar

110

175g, 6oz cream cheese
2 egg whites
25g, 1oz icing sugar

Cook the loganberries in a little water until they soften. Purée
and sieve them. Add the rosewater. Cool and then freeze the
puréed loganberries until the slushy stage. Beat the sugar and
cream cheese together and beat into the half frozen purée.
Freeze until just firm. When you are ready to serve the pudding,
allow to soften a little, whisk the egg white with icing sugar
and fold into the loganberry cream to give a swirled effect.

BLUEBERRIES - Vaccinium myrtillus

Blueberries have become very popular here and are well known
as a superfood. You can buy young plants and it is best to grow
them on in pots as they need ericaceous soil. Recommended
varieties are Earliblue, ready for cropping in July and Brigitta
with berries ripening in late August.

A good source of Vitamin C, iron and fibre, blueberries also
contain antioxidant compounds which may protect against heart
disease and some cancers. One of these is a flavonoid called
anthocyanin which gives the berries their blue colour. Like
raspberries they also contain ellagic acid, another important
antioxidant. Low in calories - 100g would give you 60 calories
- they freeze well and are a versatile berry which can be used
in sauces to accompany meat as well as in many puddings either
on their own or combined with other fruit.

BLUEBERRY AND VANILLA PAVLOVA
Serves 6 – 8

4 egg whites
225g, 8oz caster sugar
1 tsp vanilla essence
1 tsp cornflour
1 tsp white wine vinegar

Topping
225g, 8oz blueberries
25g, 1oz caster sugar
225g, 8oz mascarpone
2 tbsp light muscovado sugar
150ml, ¼pt Greek yoghurt
1 tbsp lemon juice

To make the pavlova grease a baking sheet or line it with siliconised paper. Whisk the egg whites until stiff, and continue whisking while gradually adding the caster sugar. Fold in the vanilla essence, vinegar and cornflour. Spread the mixture into a circle on the baking sheet and bake in a pre-heated oven at gas mark 4, 180°C (350°F) for 5 minutes then reduce to gas mark 1, 120°C (275°F) and cook for a further hour. Remove from the oven, cool and turn out. Put the blueberries in a small saucepan with the sugar. Heat gently until the sugar dissolves and the blueberries soften slightly. Leave to cool. Beat the mascarpone and stir in the sugar, yoghurt and lemon juice. Spread the mascarpone mixture over the pavlova and cover with the blueberries. Serve immediately.

CHERRIES
Prunus avium = sweet cherry
Prunus cesarus = sour or wild cherry

Cherries are native to Asia Minor, their name deriving from an ancient city, Cerasus where Europeans first came across them.

Cherries come in many varieties and can be divided into three groups: sweet, sour and hybrid. Sweet cherries grow on large trees and have to be cross-pollinated by other cherry trees. The sour cherries are chiefly morellos and Duke is a popular hybrid, suitable for growing in your garden.

The wild cherry is a shrub, growing about 1½m, 5ft tall with white flowers appearing before the leaves. The fruit is deep red or black and looks like a cultivated morello cherry. The gean is the tree variety of the wild cherry and grows up to 18m, 60ft.

Cherries contain vitamins A and C and some fibre. Calories vary depending on the type – sour cherries would give about 56 calories per 100g and sweet ones up to 77 calories per 100g.

The bark of the wild black cherry tree is well known as a remedy for coughs and colds. Traditionally it can be combined with dried coltsfoot leaves and flowers to cure coughs as well as feverish colds. Dry the bark in the shade. Put 2 tablespoons of dried wild cherry tree bark and 2 tablespoons of dried coltsfoot leaves or flowers in a saucepan. Bring 600ml, 1pt of water to the boil and pour over the mixture. Allow to simmer for 20 minutes. Strain, sweeten with honey and allow to cool. Take half a cup three times a day.

CHERRY CLAFOUTIS
Serves 4 – 6

75g, 3oz flour
3 eggs
300ml, ½pt milk
350g, 12oz black cherries
50g, 2oz brown sugar

Sift the flour into a bowl, make a well in the centre and drop in the eggs. Beat together, add the milk and mix until smooth. Leave to stand for 30 minutes. Heat a spoonful of oil in a baking tin until it is really hot. Pour in the batter mixture and lay the cherries on top. Sprinkle with the brown sugar and put in the oven at gas mark 7, 220°C (425°F) for about 20 minutes and then lower the heat to gas mark 5, 190°C (375°F) and cook for another 10 minutes. Serve warm with extra sugar if necessary and cream.

PLUMS - Prunus

Plum trees were introduced here from France and Italy in the 15th century. Brogdale Fruit Research Station have a plum grown from a stone found on the wreck of the warship, Mary Rose. You may have plum trees in your garden. Victoria is the most popular dessert plum and is self-fertile so worth growing; it was discovered in a Sussex wood in the 1840s. There are also culinary plums such as Czar which are tart and should be used for cooking. Plum trees do also grow in the wild. Plums are one of the earliest fruit trees to open their flowers in the spring. Greengages are like plums with sweet, greeny yellow flesh but are smaller and firmer with a deep crease down one side. The first greengage was brought to Britain by, and named after, Sir Thomas Gage who lived in Suffolk. Damsons and bullaces are related to plums but feature separately in this book.

114

PLUM VICTORIA SPONGE
Serves 6

450g, 1lb Victoria plums, halved and de-stoned
75g, 3oz granulated sugar

For the sponge
100g, 4oz self-raising flour
100g, 4oz caster sugar
½ tsp vanilla essence
100g, 4oz butter
2 eggs

Put the plums in a greased, round ovenproof dish and sprinkle with the sugar. Beat together all the ingredients for the sponge and spoon over the plums. Bake in the oven at gas mark 4, 180°C (350°F) for 25 minutes or until the sponge is cooked. Serve hot with custard or cream.

PLUM AND BLACKBERRY JAM
Makes about 4 - 5 jars

900g, 2lb Victoria plums, halved and de-stoned
350g, 12oz blackberries
1.3kg, 3lb granulated sugar
1 tbsp lemon juice
knob of butter

Put the plums and blackberries in a preserving pan and simmer gently for about 20 minutes. Then add the sugar and lemon juice and stir until the sugar has dissolved. Add the butter and bring the mixture to a boil. Boil fast until setting point is reached. Remove the pan from the heat and cool a little before pouring into warm jars.

MULBERRIES - Morus nigra

Black mulberries are native to Western Asia. The Greeks and Romans grew them – Pliny the Elder called the mulberry the wisest of trees. The Roman emperor Justinian encouraged the planting of mulberry trees in order to produce silk and the Romans brought them to Britain where they became popular in the Middle Ages. James I encouraged people to grow them and introduced large numbers to London to promote the silk industry.

There are two types of mulberry: black and white. The white mulberry produces inferior fruit but is a more decorative tree and the silk worms prefer it. Mulberries grow on medium sized trees which are slow to develop but live to a grand old age and often look gnarled. There are records showing that some mulberry trees have survived 600 years. The black mulberry produces the best fruit – rather like very dark loganberries with a pleasant but slightly acidic taste. The berries drop to the ground as they ripen in late August. Beware, though, because they stain everything they touch. Then as soon as autumn arrives the trees shed their leaves. New trees will bear fruit after about five years. You can buy mulberry trees as two or three year olds and they will look fantastic in the centre of your lawn. The type to go for is Chelsea, because it is noted for its early cropping. Mulberries are versatile and can be used for jams and jellies as well as in puddings on their own or combined with other fruits. Mulberries are very high in potassium and are a good source of calcium, phosphorus and vitamin C.

MULBERRY JAM
Makes about 2.7kg, 6lb

2kg, 4¼lb mulberries, under-ripe and unwashed
2kg, 4¼lb granulated sugar

Put the mulberries in a large saucepan, and gently heat them until the juices start to run. Leave to cook slowly for 30 minutes. Meanwhile warm the granulated sugar; this could be done in the microwave. Add the hot sugar to the mulberries and cook for another 15 minutes, or until all the sugar has dissolved. Then boil the jam on a high heat for 10 minutes. Spoon a little onto a plate and push with your finger to see if it crinkles and is jelly-like. If not boil for a few more minutes and test again until the jam has set. Leave the jam for 15 minutes and add a little knob of butter to get rid of any scum that has formed. Then pour into warmed jars and seal.

117

IN THE WILD
Wild Fruit

CRAB APPLES - Malus sylvestris

Crab apple trees can be found all over Britain in woods, hedgerows, on heaths and on roadside verges. The apples are round, yellowish green, sometimes turning bright red and can be picked from July to December. Wild crab apples are the origin of all our cultivated apples. There are also large numbers of domestic apples that have seeded themselves in the wild (often from discarded apple cores) and have reverted to a wild form or crossed with real crab apple trees. Wild apple trees, often found on roadsides are quite edible raw although often quite sharp in flavour. Crab apples, though, cannot be eaten raw but make a very good jelly since they have a high pectin content and work well added to other fruits.

SPICED CRAB APPLES

1.35kg, 3lb crab apples
750ml, 1¼pt white vinegar
800g, 1¾lb granulated sugar
1 x 7.5cm, 3in cinnamon stick
10 cloves
black peppercorns

Put the vinegar and spices into a pan and bring to the boil. Simmer for 5 minutes. Strain and add the crab apples. Simmer gently in the hot vinegar until just tender. Remove the apples with a slotted spoon and transfer to hot jars. Add the granulated sugar to the vinegar and gently heat to dissolve. Then boil rapidly until syrupy. Pour the vinegar syrup over the apples, making sure the crab apples are covered. Seal and store.

CRAB APPLE JELLY

Yield will vary depending on the juiciness of the fruit. 1kg or 2lb of sugar should yield 1.5kg or just over 3lb of jelly.

1.5kg, 3lb crab apples
water
granulated sugar
juice from 1 lemon

Put the crab apples in a saucepan with just enough water to cover them. Cook until soft and then strain through muslin overnight. Measure the liquid and allow 1kg, 2lb of sugar for every 1litre or 2pts of juice. Return to the saucepan with the sugar and lemon juice. Heat gently to dissolve the sugar and then boil until setting point is reached.

Wild Flowers, Roots and Greens

LIME FLOWERS (lime = tilea vulgaris)

The lime tree flowers in early July, producing drooping clusters of strong-scented yellow blossoms. Lime flowers can be made into fritters in the same way as elderflowers. You can also make lime blossom wine. Honey made by bees using lime flowers is known to be the best flavoured and one of the most valuable types of honey. To dry the flowers spread them out on cardboard or on a wire rack covered with a tea towel or muslin. Put them into the airing cupboard, a warm oven or bottom of an Aga until they are dry and brittle. Store in an air-tight container. These dried flowers can be used to make the well known linden tea. Pasternak wrote about an avenue of lime trees:

119

'The visitors breathe in the 'unfathomable sweetness'
This gripping scent is theme and subject,
Whereas – however well they look –
The flowerbeds, the lawn, the garden,
Are but the cover of a book.

The clustered, wax-bespattered flowers
On massive trees, sedate and old,
Lit up by raindrops, burn and sparkle
Above the mansion they enfold.'

To make the tea infuse one tablespoon of dried lime flowers in 300ml, ½pt of water for 4 minutes. Strain and drink – the tea will have a honey-like scent and is said to be soothing to the digestion and nervous system. You can flavour the tea with honey if liked.

MEADOWSWEET - **Filependula ulmaria**

Meadowsweet grows all over Britain but particularly likes wet meadows, damp woods, roadside verges, ditches and any swampy ground. It is a perennial growing up to 1m, 3ft tall. Local names are courtship-and-matrimony, meadwort (referring to the flavouring of mead) and sweet hay. The plant has a square reddish stem with fragrant creamy white flowers growing in thick clusters. The leaves are dark green, toothed and silvery grey on the underside. The leaves and flowers can be used to flavour drinks – they smell similar to woodruff – a sweet smell of fresh hay. Leaves give a refreshing almond flavour to summer soups. Wine can be made or you can make an aperitif by adding about three flowerheads and a bruised leaf to a bottle of claret – pour the wine into a jug, add the flowerheads and leaves and infuse for 2 hours. Strain and serve. You can make tea using fresh or dried meadowsweet. Infuse one fresh flowerhead and a couple of shredded fresh leaves in 240ml, 8fl oz of boiling water for 10 minutes. You can use meadowsweet to add a honeyed flavour to tart fruits. Use to sweeten gooseberries, black and redcurrants, plums and apples.

MEADOWSWEET ICE CREAM
Serves 4 – 6

300ml, ½pt double cream
1 meadowsweet flowerhead
3 egg yolks
2 tbsp honey

Warm the cream with the meadowsweet until it comes close to boiling point. Take the pan off the heat and strain the cream. Whisk the egg yolks with the honey and then whisk in the cream. Freeze until the slushy stage, and then take out and whisk a couple of times at hourly intervals to break up ice crystals. Freeze until firm.

LADY'S BEDSTRAW - Galium Verum

A sprawling, feathery, little yellow-flowered plant which is common in grassy places. Like meadowsweet the flowers give off a honey scent. Lady's bedstraw was once used as a form of rennet to curdle milk when making cheese. Use the leaves and flowers as a flavouring.

REST-HARROW - **Astragalus glycyphyllos**

This is a pretty wild plant, rather like a sweet pea with pink flowers which are evident in July. It is very common in ploughed fields and chalky grassland and in some parts of the North Country children used to dig up the roots to chew as 'wild liquorice' - this was a popular name for rest-harrow, though strictly speaking wild liquorice is another plant altogether. The roots of rest-harrow are so tough that they used to get entangled in ploughs and harrows, hence the name. It was also known as Spanish root because liquorice in the North was known as Spanish juice. The roots are black but white on the inside. It is probably best to try the roots in July when the plants are in flower and you can identify them.

WHITE HOREHOUND - **Marrubium vulgare**

White horehound is a hardy perennial and a wild herb which you can also cultivate in your garden but it doesn't blossom until two years old. It is indigenous to Britain and flourishes in waste places and on roadside verges and is particularly common in East Anglia. The plant is a branching shrubby herb with white flowers. The leaves are wrinkled and hairy. Pick leaves and flowering tops in mid summer or later in the year. For thousands of years white horehound was valued as a cough remedy. For this purpose finely chop a small handful of horehound leaves and mix with a tablespoon of honey. The leaves contain good quantities of vitamin C. In the past it was brewed and made into horehound ale.

Mushrooms

PARASOLS - Lepiota procera

Parasols are large mushrooms and have a long growing season from July until October. The cap can be anything from 10 to 25cm, 4 – 10in in diameter and is at first spherical but then opens out. Parasols grow in grass in open woods and pastures and on roadside verges. These mushrooms make great fritters. Alternatively you can wipe them clean, dip them in flour, then beaten egg and finally in breadcrumbs and deep fry them – delicious.

PARASOL FRITTERS
Serves 4

4 parasols, wiped clean
oil for frying

Batter
50g, 2oz plain flour
1 egg
150ml, ¼pt milk

Make the batter by combining all the ingredients in a food processor. Dip each parasol mushroom in the batter. Heat the oil in a large pan and fry until crisp.

CHANTERELLES - **Cantharellus cibarius**

Chanterelles are mushrooms which grow in deciduous and conifer woods, appearing from July until the first frosts. They are much sought after on the Continent and known as girolles in France. With their brilliant egg-yolk colour and smell similar to apricots, they are easy to identify and also have an unusual shape – like a funnel with a wavy margin and a short thick stem. Their only drawback is that they take longer to cook than cultivated mushrooms. Chanterelles go brilliantly with eggs.

LINGUINE WITH CHANTERELLES
Serves 4

225g, 8oz chanterelles
1 medium onion, peeled and chopped
50g, 2oz butter
3 cloves of garlic, peeled and crushed
90ml, 3fl oz white wine
250g, 9oz linguine
1 sprig of fresh thyme, chopped
4 eggs, fried
50g, 2oz extra mature Cheddar cheese, grated

Slice the chanterelles. Sauté the onion in the butter for a few minutes, add the garlic, chanterelles and after a couple more minutes pour in the wine. Simmer for 10 minutes. Cook the pasta and toss with the mushrooms and thyme. Divide between four plates and top each with a fried egg and some grated cheese.

HEDGEHOG FUNGUS
Also known as Wood Hedgehog or Pied-de-Mouton
Hydnum rapandum

The hedgehog fungus is common in woodlands, hiding in dead leaves, from August to October; it has an irregular, wavy-edged cap which is usually beige or light yellow, a short fat white stem and spines (hence the name hedgehog) instead of gills. Good to eat after blanching (slice and cook in water for a few minutes as they are a little bitter) they work well fried in butter or simmered in milk or stock.

HEDGEHOGS IN CREAM AND PAPRIKA
Serves 2 – 3

175g, 6oz hedgehogs, blanched and sliced
25g, 1oz butter
150ml, ¼pt double cream
sprinkling of paprika

Sauté the sliced hedgehogs in the butter. Stir in the double cream and the paprika. Heat through and serve.

PUFFBALLS
Giant Puffball - Lycoperdon gigantum
Common Puffball - Lycoperdon perlatum

The giant puffball can be a fantastic sight standing out from the grass and gleaming white. It can grow up to 30cm, 1ft across. Young puffballs can be spherical but older ones are more pumpkin shaped. The common puffball is much smaller, has more of a stem with a pear shape and conical thorns around the head. Only pick if still young and white. Puffballs can be found in open fields, under hedges and near compost heaps, from August until October. Puffballs are so big – you'll need to cut them up. You can slice them into steaks and fry, grill or bake them in butter or oil.

STUFFED PUFFBALLS
Serves 4

12 common puffballs
75g, 3oz butter, softened
1 medium onion, peeled and grated
2 cloves of garlic, peeled and crushed
1 tbsp breadcrumbs
1 tbsp fresh parsley, chopped
salt and pepper
a little olive oil

Slice off the bottoms of the mushrooms and scoop out the centres. Chop finely and beat into the butter along with the onion, garlic, breadcrumbs, parsley, salt and pepper. Stuff the mixture into the hollowed out shells and place on a baking tray. Drizzle a little olive oil over the puffballs and bake in the oven at gas mark 5, 190°C (375°F) for about 25 minutes or until browned.

126

On the Sea Shore

SEA PURSLANE - Halimione portulacoides

Sea purslane can be found along British coasts especially on the edges of muddy creeks or salt marshes. It is a woody perennial growing up to 80cm, 2½ft and has silvery grey oval leaves. The whole plant is covered in a grey coloured 'flour' formed by bladder-like hairs and has small yellowish-green flowers. It is a straggly many-branched plant. You will need to wear boots when collecting it. Great clumps of the plant often blanket the ground. It is best to pick the succulent leaves when young and add them to salads or boil them as you would French beans and serve with butter. You can also pickle the leaves in spiced vinegar.

EARLY AUTUMN
September

You can still sow over-wintering lettuces, autumn spinach, mustard leaves and turnips. On the vegetable front continue to pick beetroot, carrots, chard, lettuces, rocket, runner and French beans. Courgettes, cucumbers, pumpkins, squashes and tomatoes should now be ready. All are featured here along with soya beans and calabrese. From your flower border you can use the nasturtium leaves in salads. Garden fruit will be plentiful with early varieties of apples ready for picking as well as autumn raspberries and also featured in this section are pears, figs and barberries.

From the hedgerows and countryside you should now be able to gather blackberries, rowanberries, bilberries, wild damsons, elderberries and hazelnuts. Later varieties of crab apples may still be found. Greens such as good King Henry and chickweed will be available but you will have so much produce from the garden you may not need to go foraging for these. Horseradish root and wild chicory and dandelion roots are featured here as they are useful.

Mushrooms are plentiful now and include chanterelles, ceps, fairy ring mushrooms and shaggy ink caps. On the sea shore you can still pick sea beet and samphire.

I love September when fruit from the hedgerows is plentiful, the apples are ripening and there is ample opportunity to make jams, jellies and chutneys. My favourite jelly, which I make every year, is blackberry and apple – I make jars and jars of this. I also like to make a hedgerow jelly with a combination of crab apples, elderberries, sloes, haws and rosehips (sloes seem to be ready earlier each year and were ready in September last year but are traditionally picked later so I have included them under October). There is so much produce available and it means you will be kept incredibly busy. There are all the vegetables from the garden to pick and use – runner beans are always so prolific you may have a glut and need to give them away – they do need to be picked every day; the same goes for courgettes. Carrots and beetroot are easier because you can usually leave them in the ground until you want to use them.

CULTIVATED VEGETABLES

COURGETTES - Cucurbita pepo

Courgettes and marrows are closely related to squashes and pumpkins. The courgette is a variety of vegetable marrow (really just a small marrow) and is a recently introduced vegetable in comparison to others. Courgettes were introduced after the Second World War from Italy where they are known as zucchini. They had probably been brought to Italy from South America. They are relatively easy to grow and do well in grow bags. You can either buy seedlings in May from your local garden centre or grow them from seeds for transplanting once the last frosts have passed. Pick while still small. You can grow yellow-skinned courgettes but the flavour is much the same as green ones. You can also grow round courgettes – Eight Ball is the green variety and One Ball is the yellow variety – in both cases pick when the courgettes are tennis ball-sized. Courgettes have a high percentage of water and are therefore low in calories. They are a good source of Vitamin C. They are quite a versatile vegetable in the kitchen and you can use the flowers to make fritters.

COURGETTE FLOWER FRITTERS
Serves 4

12 courgette flowers
125g, 5oz plain flour
2 eggs
pinch of salt
approx 150ml, ¼pt water
oil for frying

First of all remove the pistil and small green leaves from around the yellow flowers. Lightly beat the eggs with a pinch of salt and then add the flour and whisk to get rid of lumps. Stir in the water until you have a fairly liquid mixture. Set aside for 30 minutes. Dip the courgette flowers into the batter, holding them upside down to let any surplus drain off and deep fry in oil turning them over with two forks if necessary.

COURGETTE AND GOAT'S CHEESE FLAN
Serves 6

225g, 8oz shortcrust pastry
450g, 1lb courgettes, sliced
15g, ½oz butter
3 eggs
225g, 8oz goat's cheese
1 tbsp fresh chives, chopped
1 sprig of thyme, chopped

Roll out the pastry and use to line a greased 20cm, 8in flan dish. Bake blind for 15 minutes in the oven at gas mark 4, 180°C (350°F) for 15 minutes. Fry the courgette slices in the butter for a few minutes to soften them. Whisk the eggs with the goat's cheese and herbs. Scatter the courgette slices over the pastry and pour the egg mixture over them. Return to the oven for another 25 minutes. Allow to cool a little before serving.

CUCUMBER - Cucumis sativus

Cucumbers are one of the oldest vegetables around. The first record of them was in Mesopotamia around 2000BC in the earliest known vegetable garden. We also have evidence that cucumbers were being grown in India around 1000BC. The Romans cultivated them in raised beds mounted on wheels so they could be moved around and kept in the sunshine. They were then moved under cover for the night. If you don't have a greenhouse, cold frame or cloche then you need to grow ridge cucumbers which are the hardiest. These however must be sown under protection inside preferably and then can be planted outside once the danger of frosts has passed. Many people grow cucumbers from plants bought in late May or early June. Greenhouse or indoor cucumbers are the other type of cucumber that you could grow in a cold frame if you don't have a greenhouse. If you grow ridge cucumbers the skin can be quite indigestible so these are best peeled. You need to harvest them when they are about 23cm, 9in long – regular picking will encourage more fruit to form. You should, with luck, be picking a succession of cucumbers in September. Cucumbers are useful for salads, cold soups and in various hot dishes but are actually 96% water. Their flavour is in the seeds. They contain small amounts of Vitamins A and C and potassium.

CUCUMBER AND EGG MOUSSE
Serves 6

½ a cucumber, diced
½ tsp salt
6 hard-boiled eggs, peeled
1 x 450ml, 15fl oz can jellied consommé
2 tbsp majoram, chopped
300ml, ½pt double cream, whipped
1 tbsp fresh chives, chopped
pepper

Put the diced cucumber in a colander and sprinkle with salt. Allow to drain for an hour and then pat dry with kitchen paper. Place the eggs, consommé and majoram in a food processor and purée until smooth. Fold the whipped cream and cucumber into the egg mixture, season with pepper and add the chives. Pour the mixture into a mould or soufflé dish and chill in the fridge until set.

PUMPKINS AND SQUASHES
Cucurbita maxima and moschata

Pumpkins and squashes originated in America; squashes are thought to have been cultivated for at least 5,000 years. The word pumpkin comes from the Greek word for melon – Pepon – or cooked in the sun. Squash on the other hand is an abbreviation from the North American word askutasquash meaning eaten uncooked. Wild forms were originally gathered for their seeds. Varieties of squash and pumpkins arrived in Europe after the discovery of the New World in the 1500s.

There are many varieties of both trailing and bush types and you can grow summer and winter squashes. Squashes and pumpkins come in all sorts of colours and shapes but they all taste virtually the same. It is best to grow the seeds in pots in a propagator or on a warm window-sill for transplanting when the danger of frosts has passed in May. I grew buttercup squash last year very successfully but the plants need lots of space because they trail and need a substantial amount of trimming back. They can be trailed over a trellis or you can make the trailing stems grow round a circle of pegs. To make sure you get decent-sized squashes only allow two or three per plant and you can put an old tile or piece of wood under each squash or pumpkin as they develop to stop them rotting on the soil. Once picked you can store your squashes and pumpkins for months in a cool, dry place. Nutritionally they are high in beta-carotene and also contain vitamin C and folic acid. Pumpkins and squashes are very versatile and can be used in soups and breads, can be roasted, puréed or baked in their skins or used in sweet dishes such as the traditional American pumpkin pie. Pumpkin seeds are also edible but need to be roasted; they're a good source of B vitamins, phosphorus, iron and zinc.

PUMPKIN AND TOMATO SOUP
Serves 4 - 6

2 tbsp olive oil
1 onion, chopped
½ tsp dried chilli flakes
¼ tsp cumin, ground
450g, 1lb pumpkin flesh, chopped
100g, 4oz carrots, peeled and chopped
3 tomatoes, sliced
1 clove of garlic, peeled and crushed
1litre, 2pts Marigold Swiss vegetable bouillon stock
1 tbsp fresh parsley, chopped

Heat the oil in a large saucepan and fry the onion until soft, stirring in the dried chilli flakes and cumin powder. Add the pumpkin, carrot, tomatoes, garlic and stock and bring to the boil. Simmer for 30 minutes and then liquidize the soup. Sprinkle with parsley and serve.

BUTTERNUT SQUASH RISOTTO
WITH ROCKET
Serves 4 – 6

25g, 1oz butter
1 onion, peeled and chopped
2 garlic cloves, peeled and chopped
1 medium butternut squash, peeled and cut into cubes
350g, 12oz risotto rice
1litre, 2pts Marigold Swiss vegetable bouillon stock
50g, 2oz Parmesan cheese, grated
25g, 1oz rocket leaves

Melt the butter in a large frying pan and cook the onion until softened. Add the squash and then the rice and stir around to coat with the oil. Gradually add the stock spoon by spoon, letting it be absorbed before adding more. Add the rocket and cheese when all the liquid has been absorbed. Stir and serve.

SOYA BEANS - Glycine soja

Soya beans have proved difficult to grow in Britain in the past because they need a hot summer in order to ripen but there are now two varieties, Envy and Ustie, on the market that have been bred specifically to grow in our British climate. They are a versatile vegetable because you can cook and eat the whole pod like a runner bean, you can shell the beans and use like broad beans or you can allow the beans to develop on the plant and dry them like haricot beans. To grow successfully a warm, sunny site is important. Sow beans outside in May or June. They will grow quite high and so may need supporting to keep them upright. You should be able to pick them in August – pick them while green and when you can feel the beans inside – all the pods will be ready at the same time – you can cook like whole green beans at this stage. Leave until September and the pods will look cream-coloured – shell the beans (you may need to blanch them to soften before shelling) and cook like broad beans. For drying the beans wait until the foliage has died away, pull up the whole plant, tie them together and hang in a shed to dry. Shell them and store. The beans for the risotto over the page need to be picked in September.

RISOTTO WITH GREEN SOYA BEANS
Serves 4

25g, 1oz butter
1 onion, peeled and chopped
100g, 4oz unsmoked streaky bacon, chopped
2 red peppers
350g, 12oz Arborio rice
150ml, ¼pt white wine
1 litre, 2pts Marigold Swiss vegetable bouillon stock
100g, 4oz green soya beans, cooked for 6 minutes in boiling water and drained
50g, 2oz Parmesan cheese, grated

Heat the butter in a large frying pan and cook the onion and bacon until crispy. Add the peppers and fry for a couple more minutes. Add the rice. Stir to coat in the juices and then gradually add the wine and stock, stirring all the time as the liquid gets absorbed. When the rice is tender and all the liquid has been absorbed, stir in the soya beans and cheese. Cook for a couple of minutes and serve straightaway.

TOMATOES - Lycopersicon esculentum

The tomato originated in Mexico (the word 'tomato' comes from the Mexican 'tomatl') and like the potato was brought to Europe by Spanish conquistadors. It was introduced into Europe through Italy in the 1500s. At first it was thought to be poisonous and was grown as an ornamental plant. The tomato comes from the same family as the potato and is related to the Deadly Nightshade. Like the potato the tomato has poisonous leaves. First known in Europe as 'pomme d'amour' – love apple, (which in itself must have derived from the Italian word 'pomodoro', meaning literally 'golden apple') the first tomatoes seen in Europe were small and yellow.

There are so many different varieties of tomatoes on the market and I am not going to describe them all here. Outdoor tomatoes are always grown from plants and are readily available from garden centres in late spring. Plants can be planted outside once the first flowering truss can be seen and once all risk of frost has passed. I usually grow cherry tomatoes in grow bags and they can be very successful providing we have a long, warm, sunny summer. Tomatoes should be ripening up and ready for picking from mid August through September. They contain lycopene, a carotenoid, which gives tomatoes their red colour and may help prevent prostate cancer in men and heart disease. Even tomato ketchup is therefore good for you.

TOMATO CHARLOTTE
Serves 4

1kg, 2lb tomatoes, blanched, skinned and sliced
12 thin slices white bread
75g, 3oz butter
salt and pepper
1 tsp sugar
1 tsp basil, fresh or dried
50g, 2oz mature Cheddar cheese, grated

Butter all the slices of bread on one side and cut each slice into three. Line a pie dish with the bread, butter side down. Put in a layer of tomatoes and season with salt, pepper, sugar and basil. Cover with a layer of bread, then add the remaining tomatoes, seasoning them and top with the remaining bread. Sprinkle the cheese on the top and cook in the oven at gas mark 4, 180°C (350°F) for 30 minutes. The bread should be crisp round the edges. Serve hot with any green veg or a salad.

TOMATO AND BASIL SOUP
Serves 6

2 tbsp olive oil
1 onion, peeled and chopped
1kg, 2lb tomatoes
3 tbsp plain flour
1 litre, 2pts Marigold Swiss vegetable bouillon stock
2 tbsp tomato purée
2 tsp fresh basil, chopped + salt and pepper
150ml, ¼pt single cream

Heat the oil in a saucepan and add the onions. Cook until browned and then add the flour. Gradually add the stock over a low heat and stir until thick and smooth. Stir in the tomato purée, basil and tomatoes. Cover the pan and simmer for 30 minutes. Sieve or purée in a blender, return to the saucepan to re-heat and pour into bowls, swirling a little cream over each portion.

TOMATO KETCHUP

1kg, 2lb tomatoes, skinned and chopped
2 red onions, skinned and chopped
2 eating apples, peeled, cored and chopped
2 garlic cloves, peeled and chopped
200ml, 7fl oz red wine vinegar
100g, 4oz granulated sugar
½ tsp salt
½ tsp black pepper
pinch of cayenne pepper
2 cloves
¼ tsp allspice

Put all ingredients together in a large saucepan and bring to the boil. Then turn the heat down and simmer for about an hour. Check every so often and stir if the mixture seems to be sticking to the bottom of the saucepan. Purée and or sieve the ketchup for a smooth consistency. Spoon into sterilised jars or bottles and seal. Keep in the fridge.

BEETROOT - Beta vulgaris

Beetroot as we know it today was developed by German gardeners in the Middle Ages. The Romans did grow beetroot but used it for its young leaves only realising about the value of the swollen root later on. Beetroot has only really been popular in Britain since Tudor times. It grows best in cooler regions which is why some of the best recipes come from Northern Europe and Russia in particular.

It is relatively easy to grow and you can use the leaves as you would spinach. There are various types and shapes that you can grow and they can be divided into multigerm varieties in which the corky seeds are actually fruits containing multiple seeds. These will therefore need thinning when about 2.5cm, 1in high – Boltardy and Wodan F1 are popular. Alternatively you can go for a Monogerm type which has one seed and will not need thinning – Moneta is a good choice. Sow beetroot in May and in July for a later crop. Beetroot must be handled carefully before cooking as if you pierce the skin at all the beet will bleed. Twist off the leaves carefully and don't cut off the ends! The red colour comes from the cell sap but varieties in other colours such as yellow and pink have been developed. When the beetroot is cooked and you need to peel it, it is a good idea to wear plastic gloves otherwise you will stain your hands red.

Beetroot is higher in carbohydrates than most vegetables and is a good source of folic acid and potassium. It also has a high natural sugar content, so works in cake recipes. It is particularly high in folate, a B vitamin which is necessary for normal tissue growth. The red pigmentation, betacyanin, contains anti-cancer agents. Beetroot's potential effectiveness against colon cancer has been demonstrated in several studies. The leafy tops are a source of calcium, iron and beta-carotene. There's an old wives' tale that beetroot is good for the blood - this is a myth.

CREAMY BEETROOT AND HORSERADISH

You can dig up horseradish root at this time of year.

450g, 1lb cooked beetroot, sliced
pinch of salt
25g, 1oz butter
2 tsp grated horseradish
150ml, ¼pt soured cream

Melt the butter in a frying pan and heat the beetroot through. Add a little salt and the horseradish and then the soured cream. Stir until heated through and serve with beef or as a side dish.

BEETROOT BAKED IN CREAM AND LEMON
Serves 6 as a side dish

1kg, 2lb cooked beetroot
grated rind of 1 lemon
150ml, ¼pt single cream
salt and pepper
2 tbsp breadcrumbs
1 tbsp fresh dill

Butter a shallow ovenproof dish. Slice the beetroot and arrange the slices in the dish. Sprinkle the lemon rind over the beetroot. Pour over the cream and season. Bake in the oven at gas mark

4, 180°C (350°F) for 20 minutes. Sprinkle over the breadcrumbs and put under a hot grill to finish off. Sprinkle the dill over the breadcrumbs and serve.

BEETROOT AND CHOCOLATE CAKE WITH LEMON BUTTER FILLING
Serves 8

225g, 8oz self-raising flour
1 tsp baking powder
25g, 1oz cocoa powder
100g, 4oz golden caster sugar
100g, 4oz raw beetroot, peeled
1 tsp vanilla essence
2 eggs, beaten
75g, 3oz plain chocolate
75g, 3oz butter

Filling
50g, 2oz butter
100g, 4oz icing sugar
1 tsp lemon juice
½ tsp lemon zest

Sift together the flour, baking powder and cocoa powder. Grate the beetroot using plastic gloves. Stir the sugar, grated beetroot, vanilla essence and beaten eggs into the dry ingredients. Melt the butter and chocolate together in a microwave and stir to combine before adding to the cake mixture. Spoon into two greased 17.5cm, 7in cake tins and bake in the oven at gas mark 4, 180°C (350°F) for 35 minutes or until a skewer comes out clean. To make the filling beat the icing sugar into the butter and add the lemon juice and zest. Sandwich the cakes together and sift a little icing sugar over the cake before serving.

CALABRESE - **Brassica oleracea**

Calabrese is the name for summer sprouting broccoli. It is easy to grow (sow seeds in March) and will produce one central floret. Pick this and the plant will continue to produce a steady flow of edible florets well into the winter.

CALABRESE IN CURRIED LEMON MAYONNAISE
Serves 4 as a side dish

450g, 1lb calabrese florets
1 tbsp soured cream
1 tsp curry powder

For the mayonnaise

2 egg yolks
1 tsp caster sugar
salt and black pepper
150ml, ¼pt olive oil + 150ml, ¼pt sunflower oil
3 tbsp lemon juice

Cook the broccoli in a small amount of water or steam until just tender and then drain it. To make the mayonnaise put the egg yolks, sugar and seasoning in a food processor and whiz for a few seconds. Start adding the oil, drip by drip and then in a slow steady trickle. Do not add it too fast or the mixture will curdle. When you have added about half of the oils you can add the lemon juice tablespoon by tablespoon. Then add the rest of the oil in the same way as before. If the mixture curdles you can rescue it by adding another egg yolk. Beat the extra yolk and then add the curdled mayonnaise to it very slowly, beating all the time. This should give you a smooth mayonnaise. Mix the soured cream into the mayonnaise and add the curry powder to taste. Spoon the mayonnaise over the broccoli before serving.

CARROTS - Daucus carota

The carrot originated in Afghanistan about 5,000 years ago but these carrots were purple, white, red, yellow, green or black. In Roman times carrots were purple or white. Arab merchants travelling the trade routes of Africa, Arabia and Asia brought the purple seeds home with them and then Moorish invaders probably brought the purple and yellow varieties of carrots from North Africa to Southern Europe around the 12th century. Flemish refugees eventually introduced the yellow and purple carrot to England in the 15th century. The Elizabethans used carrot tops instead of feathers to decorate their hats and brooches.

Orange carrots were developed in Holland in the 1700s by patriotic Dutchmen who wanted to grow them in the colours of the House of Orange. Pale yellow versions were crossed with red varieties which contained anthocyanin and thus produced orange-coloured roots.

Carrots sown in May will be ready in September or early October. Varieties that I would recommend are Amsterdam Forcing and Early Nantes which are short rooted early carrots (these can be sown around the end of March). For the maincrop try Chantenay, James Scarlet Intermediate and for a late crop try St Valery or Flakkee.

Carrots contain the richest source of beta-carotene which is converted by the liver in the body to vitamin A, a lack of which is alleged to cause poor night vision. They also contain anti-oxidants, helping fight against cancer and heart disease. They are rich in various minerals including sodium, sulphur, chlorine and contain traces of iodine. These minerals lie very close to the skin so if possible you should scrub the carrots to get rid of any dirt rather than peeling them. Carrots contain about 7% natural sugar and so work well in sweet recipes such as carrot cakes. Carrots are the one vegetable that do you more good if eaten cooked rather than raw as the beta-carotene is more easily absorbed when heated — cooked carrots contain up to three times more antioxidants than raw carrots.

CARROT, CHEESE AND TARRAGON SOUFFLÉ
Serves 4

450g, 1lb carrots, scrubbed and chopped
25g, 1oz butter
25g, 1oz plain flour
150ml, ¼pt milk
4 eggs, separated
50g, 2oz mature Cheddar cheese, grated
1 tsp fresh tarragon, chopped

Cook the carrots and purée them. Melt the butter in a saucepan and stir in the flour. Gradually add the milk, stirring all the time until the sauce is smooth. Stir in the carrot, the egg yolks one at a time, the carrot purée, the tarragon and the cheese. Whisk the egg whites until stiff and with a metal spoon gently fold them into the mixture. Pour into a greased soufflé dish and cook in a preheated oven at gas mark 5, 190°C (375°F) for 30 minutes. Serve immediately.

CARROT CAKE WITH
LEMON AND LIME FILLING
Serves 6

175g, 6oz wholemeal flour
2 tsp baking powder
100g, 4oz carrots, scrubbed and grated
100g, 4oz butter
100g, 4oz light brown sugar
2 eggs
2 tbsp milk

Filling
100g, 4oz cream cheese
25g, 1oz butter
grated rind of ½ a lemon and 1 lime
½ tsp vanilla essence
200g, 7oz icing sugar

You can put all the ingredients for the cake in a food processor and whiz until smooth. Alternatively sift together the flour and baking powder. Add the grated carrot. Cream the butter and brown sugar together. Beat the eggs and add to the mixture, adding a little flour if the mixture begins to curdle. Gradually add all the flour and carrot and mix in the milk. Grease two 15cm, 6in round cake tins and divide the cake mixture between the two tins. Bake in the oven at gas mark 4, 180°C (350°F) for 25 minutes. Meanwhile make the filling by beating together the butter and cream cheese. Add the grated rind and beat in the icing sugar and vanilla essence. Use this filling to sandwich the cakes together. Dust with icing sugar and serve.

ONIONS - Allium cepa

Onions are one of the oldest vegetables probably cultivated 5,000 years ago. They grew wild in various regions and they were an ideal vegetable to cultivate since they were easy to grow, transportable, kept well and could be grown in a variety of soils and climates. They may well have originated in Central Asia. The Ancient Egyptians used them extensively, fed them to their slaves working on the pyramids and buried them with the pharaohs. The onion symbolized eternity which is why they have been found in the pelvic regions, flattened against the ears and in the eye sockets of mummies. Presumably the Egyptians believed onions had antiseptic qualities which could be useful in the afterlife. The Romans were keen on them and Pliny wrote of Pompeii's onions and cabbages. The Romans probably brought onions over to England but it wasn't until the Middle Ages that they gained popularity in Britain.

Onions are easiest bought as sets and planted out in March. A good variety of red onion, Red Baron, is definitely worth growing. Shallots are also a useful type of onion to grow which you can also buy as sets. In July or August when the leaves have turned yellow you can harvest them. The shallots will have formed clusters of small bulbs growing around the central set. You should lift them and leave in the sun to dry. Then they can be divided and hung in a cool dry shed. Shallots are milder than ordinary onions and work well in stews or you can pickle them. They can also be cut into rings for salads.

When you peel an onion, the reaction of enzymes in it become exposed to the air and this causes your eyes to water. Try peeling your onions under running water as this can prevent eyes watering. The juice of the onion is antiseptic and was said to cure baldness! It contains a substance that can delay blood clotting. Onions contain small amounts of vitamins and minerals but are thought to be beneficial because they contain flavonoids which may help fight against cancer.

ONION TART
Serves 4 – 6

225g, 8oz shortcrust pastry
75g, 3oz bacon, chopped
25g, 1oz butter
450g, 1lb onions, peeled and chopped
2 eggs
150ml, ¼pt soured cream
½ tsp caraway seeds

Roll out the pastry and use to line a greased 20cm, 8in flan tin. Fry the bacon in the butter for several minutes and add the onions. Fry slowly for another 10 minutes. Add the caraway seeds. Beat the eggs and soured cream together. Scatter the bacon and onion mixture over the pastry base. Pour the eggs and cream over the top and bake in the oven at gas mark 5, 190°C (375°F) for 30 minutes.

RED ONION MARMALADE
Makes about ½kg, 1lb

6 tbsp olive oil
1kg, 2lb red onions, peeled and sliced
6 tbsp demerara sugar
4 tbsp sherry vinegar

Heat the oil in a pan, add the onions and sugar and cook for an hour, stirring every so often to prevent the onions from sticking. Add the vinegar and cook for another 30 minutes.

CULTIVATED FRUITS

PEARS - Pyrus communis

The first pears were small, hard, green fruits of the wild pear tree which can still be found all over Europe. The pear tree however has been cultivated since ancient times - Pliny, the tireless compiler of botanical information, recorded 39 varieties of pear. In England by 1842 the Horticultural Society had recorded more than 700 types. About this time, on the banks of the Loire, a pear germinated and in 1849 this tree became the first Doyenne de Comice - a pear with an excellent combination of flavour, texture and aroma. There are now over 3,000 varieties recorded.

The common pear is the pome fruit of a temperate tree of the rose family. Pears are closely related to apples and quinces. Trees resemble apple trees in many ways but their leaves are shiny and they live much longer – usually 100 years or more. You may have a pear tree already in your garden. Dwarf pyramid pear trees are popular as they can be trained as espaliers.

There are different varieties to choose from - cooking, dessert and perry pears - which produce fruit in the summer, autumn or winter. Perry pears are pressed for juice which is fermented and called Perry. Some of the best dessert pears are Comice (mentioned above) and Conference which are elongated, thin and hard, keep well and good for cooking. Williams pears are tender, juicy and develop from pale green to golden yellow when ripe - they are also good for cooking.

Pears are most abundant in September and so included here. A word of warning - they do not keep well and are probably best picked unripe and left to mature. They tend to turn from being too hard to being too ripe very quickly. Pears contain A, B and C vitamins and carbohydrates.

RED CABBAGE WITH PEARS
Serves 6 - 8

1 garlic clove, peeled and crushed
1kg, 2lb red cabbage, finely shredded
2 large pears, peeled, cored and sliced
¼ tsp ground cumin
sprinkling of salt and pepper
150ml, ¼pt chicken stock
2 tbsp lemon juice

Rub the garlic round the sides of a casserole. Spoon half the cabbage into the dish, followed by a layer of pear slices. Season with salt and pepper. Repeat the layers. Pour over the stock and lemon juice. Cover and bake at gas mark 3, 160°C (325°F) for an hour. Serve with pork or gammon.

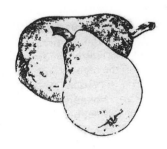

CARAMELISED BRANDY PEARS
Serves 6

6 pears, peeled
juice and rind of 1 small lemon
1 tsp ground cinnamon
175g, 6oz granulated sugar
2 tbsp brandy
1 tbsp cornflour blended to a paste with a little water

Sprinkle the lemon juice over the peeled pears and put in a saucepan. Pour in a little water. Add the grated lemon rind and cinnamon. Cover and bring to the boil. Then reduce the heat and simmer for 20 minutes. Meanwhile, put the sugar in a heavy based saucepan and heat to a golden colour. Remove from the heat and cool. Pour the liquid that the pears have been cooking in on to the caramel and stir to dissolve it over a gentle heat. Put the pears in the caramel liquid and add the brandy. Cover and cook gently for a further 10 minutes. Remove the pears and put in a serving bowl. Mix the cornflour with the water and add to the caramel liquid. Bring to the boil, and then simmer for a couple of minutes stirring all the time. Pour over the pears and serve at once.

PEAR AND GINGER TART
Serves 6

shortcrust pastry made with 225g, 8oz plain flour
and 100g, 4oz butter
3 tbsp sugar
1 tbsp preserved ginger syrup
675g, 1½lb pears, peeled, quartered and cored
2 egg yolks
2 tsp cornflour

300ml, ½pt single cream
½ tsp vanilla essence
50g, 2oz preserved ginger, drained and chopped

Roll out the pastry and line a greased 23cm, 9in flan dish, prick and bake blind in the oven at gas mark 4, 180°C (350°F) for 10 minutes. In a saucepan dissolve 1 tablespoon of sugar in 300ml, ½pt of water. Stir in the ginger syrup. Poach the pears in this syrup for 15 minutes. Drain the pears and cool. Beat the egg yolks with the rest of the sugar and cornflour. Warm the cream and stir into the egg yolk mixture along with the vanilla essence. Arrange the pears in the case, scatter over the chopped ginger and pour the custard on top. Return to the oven for 40 minutes. Allow to cool a little before serving.

FIGS - Ficus carica

Figs probably originated in Asia Minor and were one of the first fruits to have been cultivated. They were known to the Egyptians at the time of the Pharaohs and were a favoured fruit of the Greeks and Romans. In 400BC Aristophanes wrote: 'Nothing is sweeter than figs'. The Romans introduced them to Britain, planting fig trees wherever they conquered land. Figs are produced singly or in pairs in the leaf axils and are classified by the colour of their skins – there are white, purple, black and red varieties. Fig trees in England grow best in the South often up against a south facing wall. It is best to confine the root growth as this encourages fruiting. Outdoor figs try to produce two crops a year but in our climate only one crop ripens. The first crop is usually ready for picking when they are soft and when it looks as though the skin is about to split – this is usually in August or early September. The tree will also be producing tiny new figs in the autumn – these should be left and will mature the following summer. There will also be slightly larger figs that will not have time to mature before the frosts – these are the ones you should pick and discard to allow the tree to concentrate its energies on the smaller ones. Fresh figs contain 80% water and 12% sugars; however when they are dried the sugars increase to 50% - this is why dried figs are useful in cakes and puddings. The skin of fresh figs is edible. Figs are well known for their laxative properties. They are a good source of calcium, rich in iron and are high in fibre.

FIGS WITH PARMA HAM AND GINGER DRESSING
Serves 8 as a starter

8 figs
8 slices of Parma ham
25g, 1oz stem ginger
2 tbsp syrup from the stem ginger jar
3 tbsp olive oil
1 tsp lemon juice
sprinkling of black pepper

Halve the figs and arrange on a serving dish with the Parma ham draped over the figs. For the dressing, chop the stem ginger and add the syrup, oil, lemon juice and pepper. Whisk together and pour over the figs and ham.

BARBERRIES
Also known as Mahonias, Oregon Grapes or Poor Man's Redcurrant - Berberis vulgaris

Barberries are the fruit of a shrub of which many species grow wild throughout Europe, Asia and America. A closely related genus, Mahonia, is a familiar ornamental shrub. All the species bear fruits that are edible but very sour. Berries are red but vary through crimson to dark blue or black. Barberry bushes are not so often found in the wild now – the reason for this is that the berries harboured wheat rust which used to devastate arable crops and so the wild shrubs were destroyed. Nowadays various species, of which Mahonia is a popular one, can be cultivated in gardens. Mahonia berries are generally blue. Barberries used to be valued as they are high in pectin so traditional uses included preserving them in syrup or vinegar to sharpen their flavour and making them into jams and jellies. You can buy dried barberries in Middle Eastern food shops as they are popular in Iranian cookery.

IN THE WILD
Wild Fruits

BLACKBERRIES - Rubus fruticosus

Blackberries are abundant everywhere now and, although they can be picked throughout August, it is in September that people generally start thinking about blackberries which marry so well with apples. Blackberries or brambles are widespread in hedgerows and are the most commonly used wild fruit. They have been found in many of the earliest areas of habitation and were well known to the Greeks, who used the leaves for their herbal properties as well as the fruit. There is evidence that blackberries were eaten in England in Neolithic times because pips have been found in the stomach contents of a Stone Age man found preserved in clay along the Essex coast. However there are many different varieties with no single native blackberry, but instead there are hybrids so that you will notice a difference in each blackberry bush if you look carefully at the fruits or the flowers. In fact there are over 2,000 microspecies of wild blackberry. The reason for this is that they cross-pollinate very easily and birds spread the seeds in their droppings. The bushes spread because as their tips bend towards the earth they form roots. The lowest berry in each cluster, the one at the tip of the stalk, ripens first and this is the sweetest and most succulent. After a couple of weeks the other berries will ripen but these tend to be less juicy.

The dewberry is a distinct species which has smaller fruit than blackberries. These also mature earlier than most blackberries and have a matt rather than a glossy finish. Cloudberries are closely related to blackberries but in the UK are found only in Scotland.

Folklore tells us that it is unlucky to eat blackberries after 29 September (Michaelmas Day) as it is said that the devil has spat on them. In fact this date becomes 10 October in our modern calendar. This is about the time that blackberries are past their best as they become watery and tasteless.

Wild blackberries do tend to be pippy so you may wish to purée and sieve them or make large quantities of blackberry jelly. Blackberries used to be well known as a fruit eaten to help prevent scurvy. They are high in fibre and contain a wealth of minerals, including magnesium, iron and calcium. They are rich in vitamin C, potassium and are a low fat source of vitamin E. Blackberries contain bioflavonoids which act like antioxidants, protecting against cell damage.

BRAMBLE MOUSSE
Serves 6 – 8

450g, 1lb blackberries
juice of 1 lemon
3 eggs, separated
175g, 6oz caster sugar
25g, 1oz gelatine
300ml, ½pt double cream, whipped

Cook the blackberries in the lemon juice in a saucepan with a tightly fitting lid. When the brambles have softened, remove from the heat, sieve them and allow to cool. Put 3 tablespoons of water in a small saucepan and sprinkle in the gelatine. Leave to soften a little and then heat very gently until the gelatine has dissolved. Leave to cool. Whisk the egg yolks and gradually add the caster sugar, whisking until you have a thick, pale mixture. Stir in the cooled blackberry mixture and the gelatine. Add the whipped cream and lastly whisk the egg whites until stiff and fold them in too. Pour the mousse into a bowl and leave to set.

BLACKBERRY AND APPLE JELLY
Makes about 4kg, 9lb

1kg, 2.2lb cooking apples, peeled, cored and sliced
1kg, 2.2lb blackberries
water
granulated sugar

Cook the blackberries and apples together with enough water to just cover the fruit. When soft pour into muslin and suspend over a large bowl. Allow to drip through the muslin overnight and squeeze as much liquid out of the muslin as you can the next day so that you are left with just a mush of blackberry pips. Pour the blackberry and apple liquid into a large saucepan and add the sugar. For every 600ml or 1pt of juice you need 450g, 1lb of sugar. Boil rapidly until set. You can test for a set by dropping a little of the hot liquid onto a saucer. If it appears jelly-like then remove immediately from the heat. Have several jars warmed and ready and carefully pour the hot jelly into them. Leave to cool and seal well.

BLACKBERRY LIQUEUR – MURE

450g, 1lb blackberries
1 x 750ml, 1¼pt bottle of brandy
75g, 3oz granulated sugar
1 x 7.5cm, 3in stick of cinnamon
3 cloves

Whiz up the blackberries, brandy and granulated sugar in a food processor. Pour into a bottle, add the cinnamon and cloves, cork and leave for 2 months. Strain and transfer to sterilised bottles. This can be used like cassis added to wine to make a kir or to champagne to make kir royale.

ROWANBERRIES (Rowan = Sorbus aucuparia)

These are the berries of the Mountain Ash. They are a beautiful deep orange colour and hang in clusters, ready to be picked in September. You need to pick rowanberries when they are ripe – the tartaric acid in them is superseded by sugars, citric and malic acid, as the fruit ripens. Or you can pick them and allow them to ripen by storing them for a few days. The Mountain Ash is a small tree with a grey bark and toothed leaves. They make an excellent jelly to eat with game, poultry or lamb.

ROWAN JELLY

Yield will vary depending on the juiciness of the fruit. 1kg or 2lb of sugar should yield 1.5kg or just over 3lb of jelly.

1kg, 2.2lb rowanberries
300ml, ½pt water
granulated sugar
2 tbsp lemon juice

156

Wash the rowanberries and put in a large saucepan with the water. Bring to the boil and simmer until soft, crushing the berries on the side of the saucepan to help extract the juice. Strain through muslin overnight. Measure the liquid and for every litre or pint of liquid add a kilo or pound of sugar and the lemon juice. Over the heat allow the sugar to dissolve and then bring to a rapid boil. Boil until setting point is reached – this may take up to 25 minutes. Pour into warmed, sterilised jars and allow to cool before sealing.

BILBERRIES Also known as blueberries, whortleberries, huckleberries, whinberries, wineberries or hurtleberries – Vaccinium myrtillus

Bilberry bushes are most common in the North on heaths, moors and mountains on acid soils.They don't grow in the low-lying parts of Southern England and East Anglia. They are similar to blueberries but smaller. The shrubs bear tough, leathery leaves rather like those of the myrtle and turn red in the autumn. Red flowers appear in April to June and the fruit, covered with a bloom, follows from July to September. Being so small they are quite hard to pick especially as they hide under the leaves, but it is worth persevering – when you think what you pay for blueberries – these are free!

Bilberries are very juicy and can be eaten raw but work well in pies added to other fruits such as apples or pears. In Yorkshire they were made into pies known as 'mucky mouth pies' and served at funeral teas. They also combine well with mint in jams.

DAMSONS - **Prunus damascena**

Damsons came from Damascus originally and were found there by the Crusaders in the 12th century. It is thought that the Duke of Anjou brought them back to Europe after a pilgrimage to Jerusalem. Damsons are usually smaller than plums with an oval shape and blue-black fruit. The flesh is green yellow.

DAMSON AND DATE PIE
Serves 4 – 6

Shortcrust pastry made with 175g, 6oz of plain flour and
75g, 3oz butter
350g, 12oz damsons
50g, 2oz dates, chopped
100g, 4oz dark brown sugar
½ tsp ground cinnamon

Halve and stone the damsons and mix with the dates. Mix in the sugar and cinnamon. Roll out the pastry and line a greased 20cm, 8in pie dish with two thirds of the pastry. Spread the damson mixture over the pastry. Top with the remaining pastry and seal the edges. Brush with beaten egg and bake in the oven at gas mark 4, 180°C (350°F) for 25 minutes. Serve warm with cream.

DAMSON CHUTNEY
Makes 2.25kg, 5lb

450g, 1lb onions, peeled and chopped
1 clove of garlic, peeled and chopped
600ml, 1pt white malt vinegar
1 tsp mustard powder
1 tsp ground ginger + ½ tsp ground nutmeg
450g, 1lb peeled, cored and chopped cooking apples

1½ kg, 3lb damsons, halved and de-stoned
450g, 1lb granulated sugar

Put the onion and garlic in a preserving pan with half the vinegar and the spices. Simmer for 15 minutes. Add the chopped apples with the damsons and remaining vinegar. Simmer for 30 minutes and then add the sugar and stir over a low heat to dissolve. Raise the heat slightly and simmer until thick. Spoon into warm jars and seal.

ELDERBERRIES (Elder = Sambucus nigra)

Elderberries are small and black and grow in large, umbrella-like clusters which droop down as the fruits ripen. They should be picked as soon as the berries turn black but use them straightaway as they do not keep. Elderberries are very rich in vitamin C and minerals so an elderberry syrup is a perfect remedy for a cold. Elderberries have a strong flavour somewhat similar to blackcurrants.

ELDERBERRY CORDIAL

Elderberries, as many as you like, removed from stalks
cloves
granulated sugar

Put the elderberries in a large saucepan with only a little water, crush against the sides and cook slowly until soft. Strain through muslin, extracting as much juice as possible. For every 600ml, 1pt of elderberrry juice, add 450g, 1lb of sugar and 5 cloves. Return to a clean saucepan, heat until the sugar has dissolved and then simmer for 30 minutes. Allow to cool and then pour into sterile bottles, distributing the cloves between the bottles - they act as an extra preservative. Dilute with boiling water and use as a guard against colds, or as a soothing mixture when you have a cough.

HAZELNUTS - Corylus avellana

The hazel tree is probably the most widespread of nut trees in Britain. Other similar types are the filberts, which are large and oval and cobnuts which are round. Filberts were around in ancient times and the Romans probably brought them to Britain. Harvesting for filberts used to begin on 22 August, St Philbert's day.

Hazels are shrubby trees found in woods, thickets and hedgerows with the familiar yellow catkins (also known as lambs' tails). These are the male flowers, which appear in January, and in order for the tree to bear fruit, the pollen from the catkins must reach the stigmas of the female flowers (sometimes called red ladies) which are tiny and red and look like sea urchins. The problem is that the female flowers have to be pollinated by catkins from another hazel tree nearby and rely on the wind for pollination. The nuts, which are small and round and with thinner shells than commercially grown filberts and cobnuts grow in clusters of two or three, hanging down under a leaf. Apparently, before the First World War on Holy Cross Day which was 14 September, village schools used to close so that everyone could go nutting. The problem with gathering hazelnuts in the autumn is that you have to get them before the squirrels. If you pick in late August when the nuts are still on the tree they may well not be good – too soft and likely to wither in their shells. It is best to wait for the nuts to fall in September when they are ripe and brown. You will still be competing with the squirrels, birds and dormice (for which the nuts are a vital food source).

If you are thinking of planting your own hazel trees, I am afraid you have to wait for seven years before they will produce nuts. They are extremely rich in protein and calcium and are high in monounsaturated fat, the good fat that is said to lower cholesterol. They are also an excellent source of minerals such as potassium, phosphorus and magnesium.

TURKEY WITH LEMON AND HAZELNUTS
Serves 4

4 turkey breast fillets
2 eggs, beaten
175g, 6oz hazelnuts, finely chopped
75g, 3oz butter

Sauce
120ml, 4 fl oz dry white vermouth
2 tbsp lemon juice
1 tbsp fresh tarragon, chopped
75g, 3oz butter

Beat the turkey fillets with a rolling pin. Dip the turkey into the beaten egg. Spread the hazelnuts out on a plate and coat the fillets with them. Heat the butter in a large frying pan, add the turkey and fry for a couple of minutes on each side, until golden brown. Remove and keep warm. To make the sauce add the vermouth to the pan and boil until reduced by half. Add the lemon juice, tarragon and seasoning. Off the heat whisk in the diced butter to thicken. Pour over the turkey and serve.

.

OATMEAL AND HAZELNUT LOAF
Makes 1 loaf

100g, 4oz self-raising flour
½ tsp bicarbonate of soda
50g, 2oz coarse oatmeal
75g, 3oz chopped hazelnuts
2 tbsp olive oil
1 tbsp honey
150ml, ¼pt soured cream
1 egg

Sift the flour and bicarbonate of soda into a bowl. Add the oats and hazelnuts and mix well. Put the oil, honey and egg into another bowl and beat with a whisk. Add the flour mixture and stir together until smooth. Stir in the soured cream. Spoon into a greased 450g, 1lb loaf tin and leave to rest for 10 minutes before baking in the oven at gas mark 4, 180°C (350°F) for 45 minutes. Leave in the tin to cool for a few minutes and then turn onto a wire rack to cool.

Wild Roots

HORSERADISH - Armoracia rusticana

This is a perennial with large glossy, dock-like leaves. It can be found on waste ground and on roadside verges. White flowers appear between May and September. At this point you will be able to identify where the horseradish is growing. In September you can dig up the roots – you will need a spade as the roots are long and thin. Scrub them and peel away the outer brown skin before grating. Horseradish is very strong and potent and will make your eyes and nose water; so use gloves and wear a mask if you are very sensitive. Apparently the prefix 'horse' means 'coarse'. If you have a good quantity of horseradish you could use a food processor with a grater disc. To preserve grated horseradish, pack into jars and cover with white wine vinegar. You will need about 300ml, ½pt of vinegar for 450g, 1lb of grated horseradish. Seal the jars and store in a cool, dark place – it should keep for six months.

QUICK HORSERADISH SAUCE

1 tbsp grated horseradish
200ml, 7fl oz crème fraîche
1 tsp granulated sugar
½ tsp mustard powder
1 tsp white wine vinegar
Salt and pepper to taste

Mix the horseradish into the crème fraîche along with the sugar, mustard powder, vinegar, salt and pepper.

HORSERADISH BECHAMEL SAUCE

25g, 1oz butter
2 tbsp plain flour
200ml, 7fl oz milk
200ml, 7fl oz Marigold Swiss vegetable bouillon stock
2 tbsp double cream
3 tbsp grated horseradish

Melt the butter, stir in the flour and gradually stir in the milk and stock. Add the cream, and horseradish and serve with beef.

MACKEREL AND HORSERADISH PATÉ

3 smoked mackerel fillets
3 tbsp crème fraîche
1 tbsp grated horseradish
1 tbsp white wine vinegar
grated rind and juice of 1 small lemon
2 tbsp fresh parsley, chopped

Put all the ingredients in a food processor and process until smooth.

WILD CHICORY AND DANDELION ROOTS

You can eat the leaves of wild chicory but in the autumn you can dig up some chicory and dandelion roots and try making a coffee substitute. The roots should be scrubbed clean and then dried on a radiator or in the airing cupboard for a day. Then cut the roots into chunks and roast them in the oven at gas mark 4, 180°C (350°F). Grind the roasted roots up and either mix them together or try the ground roots of each separately as a substitute for coffee. Chicory is bitter but can be added to ordinary coffee. Dandelion coffee is not so bitter but doesn't really taste like coffee. These mixtures apparently stimulate the general metabolism and improve the function of the liver. They don't contain caffeine so will not cause sleeplessness.

Wild Flowers

POPPY SEEDS

The Romans must have known about poppies because Ceres, the corn goddess, is depicted with a bunch of poppies in her hand. The seed heads of both field and garden poppies start to dry in September. Field poppies grow along the edges of cornfields and on roadside verges. You can pick them and extract the seeds by shaking them out of the holes (these are vents through which the seeds would normally escape). Use poppy seeds in cakes, bread and biscuits.

Mushrooms

In September you should still be able to pick chanterelles, ceps and fairy ring mushrooms. Shaggy ink caps will be springing up. You should now also see field and horse mushrooms cropping up in pastures, especially those grazed by horses.

FIELD AND HORSE MUSHROOMS
Agaricus campestris and arvensis

The field mushroom looks like a cultivated mushroom but smells stronger. It is white with a short stem. The cap is domed when young, becoming flatter with age. The gills are pink to start with becoming brown. Field mushrooms are common in fields and pastures, and given the right conditions of temperature, moisture and soil condition these mushrooms can crop up overnight. Horse mushrooms are similar to field mushrooms – they can be very large, with white caps that go yellow with age. The gills are greyer than field mushrooms. Do not confuse with the poisonous yellow-staining mushroom which bruises to a bright yellow.

MUSHROOM KETCHUP

1½kg, 3lb field or horse mushrooms
100g, 4oz salt
1 tbsp pickling spice
300ml, ½pt white wine vinegar
300ml, ½pt red wine
1 small onion, peeled and chopped

Break up the mushrooms and layer in a large earthenware dish, sprinkling salt on each layer. Leave for three days in a cool place, stirring every day. Boil the vinegar with the pickling spice and onion for 15 minutes and after leaving for 24 hours, strain it. Add the mushrooms to the spiced vinegar and simmer over a low heat until well reduced for about 2 hours. Leave to cool and then pot and leave for four weeks to mature. This ketchup should keep well due to the salt and vinegar which act as preservatives.

MUSHROOM CROUSTADE
Serves 4 – 6

75g, 3oz brown breadcrumbs
75g, 3oz almonds, flaked
75g, 3oz ground almonds
1 small onion, peeled and grated
75g, 3oz butter, melted
1 clove of garlic, peeled and crushed
450g, 1lb field or horse mushrooms, sliced
25g, 1oz butter
200ml, 7fl oz crème fraîche
pinch of nutmeg

Mix together the breadcrumbs, flaked and ground almonds, onion, garlic and melted butter. Press into a greased 20cm, 8in flan dish and bake at gas mark 4, 180°C (350°F) for 15 minutes. Meanwhile fry the mushrooms in the butter for 10 minutes until all the liquid has evaporated. Spoon the mushrooms on top of the pastry base and swirl the crème fraîche over the top, adding a pinch of nutmeg. Return to the oven for 10 minutes. Serve warm.

STUFFED MUSHROOMS
Serves 4

4 large parasols, or other large mushrooms
2 tbsp olive oil
2 rashers smoked streaky bacon, chopped
1 clove of garlic, peeled and crushed
100g, 4oz white breadcrumbs
1 tsp fresh chives, chopped
50g, 2oz mature Cheddar cheese, grated
2 tbsp single cream
1 tbsp lemon juice

Cut the stalks from the mushrooms and chop them up. Fry the mushrooms in the oil for a couple of minutes to brown the caps. Remove to a baking dish. Add the bacon to the frying pan and fry along with the chopped stalks and garlic. Transfer to a bowl and mix in the breadcrumbs, chives, cheese, cream and lemon juice. Divide between the mushroom caps. Drizzle over a little more oil. Bake in the oven at gas mark 5, 190°C (375°F) for 20 minutes. Serve at once.

SHAGGY INK CAPS - **Coprinus comatus**

These are common in fields, on lawns, roadside verges, on the edges of woods and waste ground. Also known as lawyer's wigs, they look like limp umbrellas – the caps are egg-shaped to start and then look more like a bell, with large shaggy scales. Shaggy ink caps are white at first but darken to pink and then black, dissolving into an inky fluid when old. Pick them when young, before the gills start to go black and use straightaway.

SHAGGY INK CAP CREAMY SOUP
Serves 4 – 6

225g, 8oz wild mushrooms, including some shaggy ink caps
1 onion, peeled and sliced
75g, 3oz butter
40g, 1½oz plain flour
900ml, 1½pts Marigold Swiss vegetable bouillon stock
150ml, ¼pt single cream
1 tbsp fresh parsley, chopped

Chop the mushrooms up and sauté in the butter along with the onion. Stir in the flour and cook for a couple of minutes. Add the stock, cover and simmer for about 10 minutes. Liquidize and stir in the cream. Add the parsley and serve at once.

MID AUTUMN
October

At this time of year you could plant garlic, broad beans and crowns of rhubarb. Pick spinach, chard, radicchio, endive and mustard leaves. You may still have runner and climbing French beans that you can also gather and you may still have some carrots and beetroot. Swiss chard is at its best now so features here.

I love October because there are apples to harvest and quinces. Even if you don't have any apple trees in the garden you can go scrumping or look out for apple trees bearing fruit on roadside verges. These trees, called Wildings, will produce fruit that you can at least use in cooking.

In the wild it's a great time of year for wild fruits and nuts. You can find plentiful supplies of rosehips and haws, sloes, bullaces and also possibly wild service berries (chequerberries), walnuts and sweet chestnuts. Sea beet will still be growing on sea shores. For mushrooms it's still a good time of year - wood and field blewits, parasols, saffron milk caps, horn of plenty, oyster mushrooms and honey fungus should all be lurking in the fields and woods (some of these feature under the section in November).

CULTIVATED VEGETABLES

WINTER SPINACH, PERPETUAL SPINACH, SWISS CHARD - Spinacia oleracea and Beta vulgaris

Winter spinach, perpetual spinach (also known as spinach beet) and Swiss chard are very useful at this time of year when other green vegetables are over. If you plant some winter spinach in August you should be able to pick leaves from October through until the next April. Swiss chard and spinach beet can be planted in the spring but will last well through the year and are particularly useful in the autumn – both are perennials which will run to seed in the second year. You can use the stalks from Swiss chard separately from the leaves.

CHARD WITH CREAMY TOMATO SAUCE
Serves 4 – 6

*Handful of chard stalks, green leaves stripped away and
reserved to cook as spinach
200ml, 7 fl oz béchamel sauce
150ml, ¼pt fresh tomato sauce
2 tbsp mature Cheddar cheese, grated
2 tbsp brown breadcrumbs*

Slice the chard stalks and cook in boiling, salted water for 10 minutes. Mix together the white béchamel and tomato sauce. Put the chard stalks in a dish. Cover with the sauce. Sprinkle grated cheese and breadcrumbs on top and finish off under the grill.

CULTIVATED FRUITS

APPLES - Malus domestica

'No Fruit is more to our English taste than the Apple. Let the Frenchman have his Pear, the Italian his Fig, the Jamaican may retain his farinaceous Banana and the Malay his Durian, but for us the Apple.' From *'The Anatomy of Dessert' by Edward Bunyard.*

Although several varieties of apples are ready in August and

September, October is the traditional time for apples. Apple Day takes place every year on 21st October. Britain produces some of the finest apples in the world since our climate is perfect for apple trees – plenty of rain to swell the fruit, not too hot for slow ripening, ordinary English sun to colour the fruit and coolish nights to sort out the flavour. Apples are probably the most versatile of our fruits, with many, many varieties available, both for eating and for cooking. Brogdale in Kent is the home of the British National Fruit Collection and there are over 3,000 named varieties of apple.

Apples and orchards are really splendid symbols of our country and it is such a pity that so many orchards have been done away with in the last 50 years. The 80,000 hectares of land devoted to growing fruit before the war has now shrunk to 20,000 hectares. Only a very small percentage of the original ancient orchards with really interesting old varieties of English apples remain. In the past every county and in some places every village had its own variety of apple, named after the relevant person or place – for example the Lady Henniker apple which was named after Lady Henniker was developed on the Thornham Magna Estate, near Eye in Suffolk; the Duke of Devonshire was raised at Holker Hall in Lancashire, home of the Duke of Devonshire; Ribston Pippin was discovered at Ribston Hall, near Knaresborough in Yorkshire.

No other fruit has such a wide range of tastes, textures, colours, shapes and aroma. Gardeners of the past were also clever at planting a variety of apple trees to ensure a succession of apples through from late summer until the end of the year with late ripening varieties able to be stored well into the next year.

Some of the best eaters, ripening at different times are: AUGUST: Beauty of Bath and Tydeman's Early Worcester (a cross between Worcester Pearmain and McIntosh);

SEPTEMBER: Sunset (my favourite because it is so tasty), Ellison's Orange which has an aniseed flavour or Egremont Russet (this is also a commercial russet); OCTOBER: Ashmead's Kernel (raised in Gloucester by Dr Ashmead) this is one of the highest quality late dessert apples which is aromatic, sweet, juicy and refreshing; Ribston Pippin and Kidd's Orange Red (this is a cross between a Cox's Orange Pippin and Golden Delicious); NOVEMBER: Tydeman's Late Orange (a cross between Laxton's Superb and Cox) and Sturmer Pippin which produces quite tart but juicy apples – I left mine on the tree until December and they stored really well. If you want to plant some apple trees to produce eaters there is a huge choice of varieties to choose from – above I have listed some of the varieties which I think have the best taste.

Apples can be used in many recipes both sweet and savoury. Cookers have a higher acid content – Bramley is the best known but there are other varieties such as Howgate Wonder which are perfect for apple purée. Cookers were also developed with different ripening times. The first apples of the season in the past were the Keswick Codlins which would be picked in August, (they cooked to a soft juicy fluff so were ideal for soufflés); The next to ripen was the Charles Ross in September (now used as a dual purpose apple), Blenheim Orange which ripened in October along with Golden Noble and then Belle de Boskoop which was late ripening and could be left on the tree until November; the aforementioned Howgate Wonder and Edward VII also ripened late and were stored, because they were at their most flavoursome, not when picked, but after two or three months in storage.

The first cookbook I wrote was *The Apple Cookbook*, such is my love of apples. Here are just a few ideas – these are recipes I make over and over again in the autumn.

AUTUMN CHICKEN
Serves 4

This makes a tasty casserole. Serve with baked potatoes.

4 free range chicken breasts
2 tbsp sunflower oil
2 onions
225g, 8oz mushrooms
1 cooking apple, peeled, cored and chopped
300ml, ½pt apple juice
300ml, ½pt chicken stock
1 bay leaf
black pepper, freshly ground
parsley
croutons (optional)

Heat the oil in a casserole. Fry the chicken until golden brown. Remove to a plate. Fry the onions, mushrooms and apple for 5 minutes. Return the chicken and add the apple juice and stock. Add the bay leaf and some freshly ground black pepper. Cover and cook in the oven at gas mark 4, 180°C (350°F) for 1½ hours. If you want to thicken the sauce, mix a little cornflour with water and add to the casserole and cook for a further 5 minutes. Garnish with parsley and croutons.

APPLE AND ALMOND PUDDING
Serves 4 - 6

450g, 1lb cooking apples, peeled, cored and sliced
3 tbsp honey
2 tbsp water
50g, 2oz breadcrumbs
100g, 4oz caster sugar
50g, 2oz ground almonds
1 egg, beaten
75g, 3oz butter, melted

Put the apples, honey and water into a pan and cook until the fruit is soft. Stir in the breadcrumbs and place in a shallow ovenproof dish. Put the sugar, ground almonds and egg in a bowl and pour on the melted butter. Mix well and spread over the apple mixture. Bake at gas mark 5, 190°C (375°F) for 45 minutes. Bake for a little longer if the almond topping is not set. Serve hot with cream or crème fraîche.

APPLE AND RASPBERRY SCRUMBLE

Crumble
50g, 2oz plain flour
50g, 2oz oats
50g, 2oz ground almonds
75g, 3oz butter
50g, 2oz brown sugar

Filling
450g, 1lb cooking apples, peeled, cored and sliced
225g, 8oz raspberries
100g, 4oz caster sugar
3 tbsp water

Put the flour and oats in a bowl with the ground almonds. Add the butter and rub with the fingertips until the mixture resembles breadcrumbs. Stir in the brown sugar. Put the sliced apple in a pie dish with the raspberries, caster sugar and water. Pile the crumble mixture on top of the fruit and press down lightly. Bake in the oven at gas mark 4, 180°C (350°F) for 30 minutes until the crumble topping is golden brown.

APPLE CINNAMON SLICES

These slices have a flapjack like texture and are really quite delicious. The children love them.

150g, 5oz self raising flour
175g, 6oz porridge oats
175g, 6oz soft brown sugar
1 tsp ground cinnamon
175g, 6oz butter or margarine, melted
2 medium cooking apples, peeled, cored and sliced

Combine flour, oats, sugar and cinnamon. Then add the melted butter or margarine and mix thoroughly. Put half the mixture into a greased 27.5 x 17.5cm, 11 x 7in baking tin, and press down. Cover with sliced apples and then with the rest of the mixture. It may be quite difficult to spread this on top of the apples. Press it down and smooth the top with a spatula. Bake in the oven at gas mark 4, 180°C (350°F) for 25 minutes. Allow to cool before cutting into slices.

QUINCES - Cydonia vulgaris

Originally from Persia and Turkestan, quinces were popular with the Greeks and Romans. The quince features as the golden apple in Greek myths and was dedicated to Aphrodite, being the symbol of love and happiness. The golden apples of Hesperides were thought to have been quinces. The Greeks believed that the trees sprang up wherever Aphrodite stepped when she came out of the foaming sea. In the Jewish religion it is believed that the serpent tempted Eve with a quince rather than an apple. A wild version of the quince can still be found in Iran. It is a member of the rose family and bears a golden yellow fruit shaped rather like a fat pear. The flesh is hard and granular and cannot be eaten raw. The fruit has a strong and pleasant aroma and should be stored separately from other fruit. When cooked the flesh turns pink and soft.

Quinces make great jelly and a wonderful fruit cheese of which the Spanish version is called membrillo. They combine well with apples and pears in fruit puddings. Quinces are eaten in the Middle East with meat, such as lamb or chicken. Indeed in Persian cookery quinces have featured for at least the last 2,000 years in sweet and savoury dishes. It is known that quinces were being grown in Britain during the time of Edward I as he planted four trees at the Tower of London. In the early 1600s John Tradescant brought the 'Portugal' quince to Britain and the fruits were popular from then on until going into decline in the 1900s. However they are now making a comeback and the Brogdale Horticultural Trust have a 4 acre commercial quince orchard featuring 19 different varieties.

The quince tree makes a very attractive tree in the garden with beautiful pale pink blossom in May. It is a small, spreading deciduous tree which is long-lived and develops knotted, interesting-looking branches. The trees are self-fertile with single trees in gardens bearing good crops of fruit. As the fruit ripens it changes from green to yellow. The quince contains a great deal of pectin especially when it is slightly unripe, so can be combined with other fruits to make jams.

Quinces are high in potassium and vitamin A. They are rich in soluble fibre and are known to calm the stomach and allay nausea.

QUINCE CHEESE

This is called 'pasta de membrillo' in Spain or 'contignac'. You can cut the paste into small squares and roll them in icing sugar if liked.

900g, 2lb peeled and cored unripe quinces
300ml, ½pt water
granulated sugar

Cut the quinces into small pieces and put them in a large saucepan with the water. Bring to the boil and then simmer for 30 minutes until the fruit is soft. Pass through a sieve and measure the purée. Add an equal amount of sugar and cook slowly stirring until the purée thickens and forms a thick paste. It will bubble away, exploding and popping as it does so but you do need to keep stirring it as otherwise it will burn. Eventually it will be so thick that it will separate as you draw a knife through it. Pour on to greaseproof paper in a baking tray and leave to dry and set. Cut into squares and store in airtight containers. This fruit cheese keeps for ages.

APPLE AND QUINCE JELLY
Makes 1.5kg, 3½lb

This goes well with meat such as lamb and pork or can be eaten with butter and toast. If the quinces are unripe the pectin content will be higher and the lemon juice is not quite so necessary. The apples contain good quantities of pectin. The jelly is good spread on scones or as a filling for cakes but can also be served as an accompaniment for savoury dishes.

1kg, 2.2lb quinces, chopped
1.5kg, 3lb apples, chopped
granulated sugar
juice of 1 lemon

Combine the apples and quinces (including skin and cores) in a large saucepan with just enough water to cover them. Cook until the fruit is soft. Strain through a muslin bag overnight. Measure the liquid and for every 600ml, 1pt of liquid add 450g or 1lb of sugar. Add the lemon juice and over the heat allow the sugar to dissolve and then bring to a rapid boil. Boil until setting point is reached – this may take up to 25 minutes. Pour into warmed, sterilised jars and seal.

IN THE WILD
Wild Fruits

ROSEHIPS - Rosa canina

Rosehips are found everywhere in hedgerows and on roadside verges. Pick them when they are fully ripe in October. They are rather fiddly and time consuming to pick as the stems are thorny. They are also a bit of a pain to cook because of their tiny hairy pips which need to be extracted. They are therefore best used for making syrup or jelly. Rosehips are very high in Vitamin C and were collected on a huge scale during the Second World War to make syrup. You can also pour boiling water on a bowl of crushed rosehips – allow to steep for 10 minutes, then strain, add honey to taste and use as a hot drink.

APPLE AND ROSEHIP JELLY

Yield will vary depending on the juiciness of the fruit 1kg or 2lb of sugar should yield 1.5kg or just over 3lb of jelly.

1.5kg, 3lb apples
675g, 1½lb rosehips
granulated sugar

Chop up the apples without peeling or coring them and put into a large preserving pan with the rosehips. Just cover with water and bring to the boil. Simmer crushing the rosehips against the sides of the pan to release the flesh until the apples are soft. Strain the fruit through a muslin bag overnight. Measure the liquid and for every 600ml, 1pt of liquid add 450g or 1lb of sugar. Over the heat allow the sugar to dissolve and then bring to a rapid boil. Boil until setting point is reached – this may take up to 25 minutes. Pour into warmed, sterilised jars and seal.

ROSEHIP SYRUP
Makes about 1.5 litres, 2½pts

1kg, 2.2lb rosehips
2½ litres, 4½pts water
450g, 1lb granulated sugar

Wash the rosehips and remove all the stalks. Process briefly in a food processor. Put them into a saucepan with half the water, bring to the boil and boil for 20 minutes. Strain through a muslin bag, leaving the juice to drip through for at least 2 hours. Then take the rosehips and boil with the remaining water for 15 minutes. Strain the liquid again. You should have about 1 litre, 1¾ pints – add the sugar and stir over a low heat until the sugar has dissolved. Increase the heat and boil for 10 minutes. Pour into warmed, sterilised bottles and seal. Stand the bottles on a folded cloth in a deep pan, filling it with water up to the necks of the bottles. Bring to the boil and boil for 10 minutes. This should help preserve the syrup. Store in a cool dark place. Once opened the bottles of syrup will not keep for more than a few days.

HAWS - Crataegus monogyna

Hawthorns are prolific all over Britain showing up on the edges of fields, in hedges, woodland edges, scrubland and on roadside verges. The hawthorn is a deciduous shrub or small tree, also called the May tree. The hawthorn features in folklore and was said to have healing powers with the tree offering protection against lightning. The hawthorn is meant to be a symbol of life and rebirth. Some say that Christ wore a crown of hawthorn.

You can pick the young leaves in April and use them in salads. These young leaves used to be known to children as 'bread and cheese'. The hawthorn produces an abundance of strongly scented white or pink blossom in May. The leaves are deeply lobed on spiny branches. In the autumn hawthorn berries or haws can be picked and used in jellies. Haws are probably the most abundant berries at this time of year, each bush producing bunches of round, dark red berries and they last well into January. They are fiddly to pick and destalk and are quite a dry fruit, with a large pip, so need quite a lot of water which they absorb when you cook the fruit for a jelly.

HAW JELLY

Yield will vary depending on the juiciness of the fruit 1kg or 2lb of sugar should yield 1.5kg or just over 3lb of jelly. This makes a beautiful red jelly.

1kg, 2lb haws
1 litre, 2pts water
juice of 1 lemon
granulated sugar

Wash and get rid of as many of the stalks on the haws as possible. Put in a large pan with the water and simmer for 1 hour. The berries will absorb a lot of water. Pour into a muslin bag and allow to strain overnight. Do not squeeze the bag, as you will then not get a clear jelly. Measure the juice and for every 600ml, 1pt of liquid add 450g or 1lb of sugar. Return the haw juice to the pan and add the granulated sugar. Add the lemon juice and heat gently until the sugar dissolves, then boil rapidly until the jelly will set. Pour into warmed jars and seal.

SLOES - **Prunus spinosa**

These are the dark berries of the blackthorn, a thorny shrub which grows wild throughout Europe and is also native to North Africa and Asia. The stones from sloes have been found on prehistoric sites so they have obviously been useful in the diet of Early Man. The sloe is the ancestor of all cultivated plums. These shrubs are most often found in the hedgerows, growing up to 3m, 9ft high. They have long thorns and oval leaves and small white flowers appear before the leaves. The fruits resemble tiny plums and have blue-black skins. The juicy green flesh is very acid and can't be eaten raw. Sloes ripen in the autumn but are best picked after the first frosts as this softens the skin.

APPLE AND SLOE JELLY

Yield will vary depending on the juiciness of the fruit. 1kg or 2lb of sugar should yield 1.5kg or just over 3lb of jelly.

450g, 1lb sloes
900g, 2lb apples, chopped
granulated sugar

Put the sloes and apples in a preserving pan and just cover with water. Cook until the fruit is soft, crushing the sloes against the side of the pan to release their juices. Strain overnight through muslin. Measure the liquid and for every 600ml, 1pt of liquid add 450g or 1lb of sugar. Over the heat allow the sugar to dissolve and then bring to a rapid boil. Boil until setting point is reached – this may take up to 25 minutes. Pour into warmed, sterilised jars and seal.

SLOE GIN

225g, 8oz sloes
125g, 5oz caster sugar
70cl bottle of cheap gin
few drops of almond essence

Prick the sloes with a fork and put into a 1 litre, 2 pint Kilner jar. Add the sugar and pour in the gin. Add the almond essence, cover and shake the jar well. Leave in a cool, dark place for at least three months. Give the jar a shake once a week. Then strain off the sloes. Pour the liqueur into a bottle and store it until needed.

BULLACES - Prunus institia

Bullaces are the wild ancestors of plums and are native to Europe and Asia. They were grown by the Romans and Anglo Saxons and were popular in medieval orchards. The bullace makes a large bush or small tree which has some thorns but less than you would find on a sloe bush. The bluey black bullaces known as Black Bullaces are similar to sloes but slightly larger. There are also greeny yellow ones, known as Shepherd's Bullaces. The fruits are round and very bitter like sloes and so are not usually eaten raw. The flesh is yellow. A third variety, White Bullace has small, flattened fruits and a yellow skin mottled with red – these are sweeter than the other types. Bullaces ripen later than damsons in November. They grow in hedgerows and on the edges of woods. Bullaces are, like plums, high in potassium, a good source of vitamin A and contain small amounts of calcium and magnesium.

BULLACE RELISH
Makes about 1kg, 2lb

675g, 1½lb bullaces, halved and de-stoned
225g, 8oz cooking apples, peeled, cored and diced
225g, 8oz onions, peeled and minced
100g, 4oz carrots, peeled and diced
300ml, ½pt cider vinegar
225g, 8oz brown sugar
2 tsp salt
½ tsp ground cinnamon
½ tsp ground ginger
½ tsp nutmeg
½ tsp ground cloves

Put the bullaces, apples, onions and carrots in a large saucepan with half the vinegar and simmer for about 40 minutes until the fruit is soft. Add the rest of the vinegar with the sugar, spices and salt. Continue cooking, stirring every so often until the relish is thick. This should take about an hour. Pour into warm jars and seal.

WILD SERVICE BERRIES
Also known as Chequerberries
(Wild Service Tree = Sorbus torminalis)

You can use the berries from the Wild Service tree to make jelly. These are ready to pick in October and, rather like medlars, are better half rotten, preferably having been subjected to one or two frosts. Make a jelly with them following the recipe for rowan jelly on page 156.

AZAROLE Also known as Mediterranean Medlar
Crataegus azarolus

The azarole is a relation of the hawthorn but a member of the rose family. Trees can be found in the wild in hedges or on verges but in the past were also grown as ornamental garden trees. The fruit look like larger versions of haws and can be yellow, orange or bright red - they have apple-flavoured, pasty flesh - try combining with apples and making a jelly with them. These are grown commercially and the fruit used for flavouring liqueurs.

SEA BUCKTHORN - Hippophae rhamnoides

This is an attractive ornamental shrub that grows wild near the coasts of Britain but often in inaccessible places such as rocky cliff sides. Sea buckthorn flowers in April, has small, silvery leaves and produces bright orange berries towards the end of September. These stay on the bush through October and into the winter months as birds find them unpalatable – the berries are surrounded by sharp thorns so rather difficult to pick. The berries are very rich in vitamins C and A; they are very acid but can be used to make jellies and jams. The berries are such an exceptional source of health-giving nutrition that they are used commercially in products such as creams, soaps and teas.

They grow well in colder climates in Northern Europe and are widely used in Russia. You can buy plants to grow in your garden; they can be used as part of a new hedge. You need to buy two plants – one female and one male as the berries are only produced on the female plant if a male plant is nearby for pollination.

WALNUTS - **Juglans regia**

Walnut trees are native to Western Asia and were very popular with the Greeks and Romans. The Greeks used to dedicate them to the goddess Diana. They were introduced into Britain 500 years ago. Walnut trees are slow growing but make huge trees and can be found scattered around old woods and parks. The leaves and husks have been used as brown dyes and the oil used as a hair darkener or for paints. Walnut wood was much prized in the past and for this reason walnut trees growing in the wild are quite hard to find.

Young walnuts can be picked in July and pickled in their green outer covering. Make up a brine using 175g, 6oz salt to 1 litre, 2 pints of water. Wear gloves and prick the walnuts with a skewer. Put the walnuts in the brine and make up a fresh solution of brine every day for a week. Remove the walnuts and dry in a sunny place until they go black. Then pack them in jars covering them with hot pickling vinegar. Seal the jars and leave for a month before using.

Otherwise walnuts are ready for harvesting in October. You have to get rid of the green outer husk and the inner shell. When you peel the outer husks off your walnuts, unless you wear gloves, your hands will be stained yellow. Walnuts are very nutritious and despite being high in calories, eaten in small quantities are very good for you. Walnuts are unique because they contain omega 3 and omega 6 polyunsaturated fatty acids. These essential fatty acids reduce the risk of heart disease by helping to lower harmful cholesterol. They are a valuable source of phosphorus.

MACKEREL AND WALNUT PATÉ
Serves 6

450g, 1lb fresh mackerel grilled, skin and bones removed
1 clove of garlic, peeled and crushed
juice and rind of 1 lemon
225g, 8oz medium fat cream cheese
1 tbsp chopped chives
50g, 2oz walnuts, toasted and broken into small bits

Put the mackerel in a food processor and add the garlic, lemon juice and rind and whiz until smooth. Add the cream cheese and chives and process again. Lastly fold in the walnuts.

BLACK TREACLE AND WALNUT BREAD
Makes 1 large loaf

450g, 1lb plain flour
4 tsp baking powder
50g, 2oz soft brown sugar
100g, 4oz chopped walnuts
1 egg, beaten
3 tbsp black treacle, warmed
120ml, 4fl oz milk

Sieve the flour with the baking powder. Add the sugar and walnuts. Mix in the egg, warmed treacle and milk. Grease a 1kg, 2lb loaf tin and fill with the mixture. Leave to stand in a warm place for 20 minutes and then bake in the oven for 1 hour at gas mark 4, 180°C (350°F). Turn out and serve sliced with butter.

SWEET CHESTNUTS - Castanea sativa

The sweet chestnut tree originated in the Eastern Mediterranean – the Greeks introduced the trees into Europe and the Romans brought them to Britain. Trees are tall and upright with long pointed serrated leaves and the fruits, usually three together, are enclosed in round green spiky cases. Trees can be found in parks and on the edges of woods. The nuts ripen in October/November and will fall off the tree – gather the nuts and prize them from their husks. Slit the brown shells before you cook them to prevent them exploding. They cannot be eaten raw unlike other nuts. You can either boil, roast or grill them. They have a soft, floury texture and can be used in both sweet and savoury dishes. The Romans ground chestnuts into flour and the Italians used chestnut flour to make polenta before maize was introduced in the early 16th century. Nowadays Spain is the main exporter of the sweet chestnut. The word chestnut comes from the Greek 'Castanea', named after a city in ancient Asia Minor. Chestnuts are low in oil and are therefore lower in calories than other nuts but high in carbohydrates. They are also high in potassium. Chestnuts are used to make marrons glacés which are crystallized.

CHESTNUT PURÉE

To make chestnut purée you must slit the shells and then boil the chestnuts for about 10 minutes. Allow to cool before peeling off the shells and inner skin. Simmer the nuts for a further 40 minutes in a little liquid and then purée in a food processor or chop finely. To make sweetened purée make a sugar syrup using 350g, 12oz of granulated sugar to 600ml, 1pt of water. Dissolve the sugar in the water over a gentle heat, add 450g, 1lb of peeled chestnuts and a teaspoon of vanilla essence. Boil until the chestnuts are soft. Remove the chestnuts and mash them up, then mix in enough of the sugar syrup to make a soft consistency.

CHOCOLATE AND CHESTNUT CAKE
Serves 8

75g, 3oz plain chocolate
2 tbsp water
4 eggs, separated
225g, 8oz caster sugar
350g, 12oz chestnuts, cooked and sieved

Filling
150ml, ¼pt whipping cream

Melt the chocolate with the water over a pan of simmering water. Add the egg yolks and sugar and beat until thick. Whisk the egg whites and fold in with the chestnuts. Turn into a greased 20cm, 8in cake tin and cook at gas mark 4, 180°C (350°F) for 30 minutes. Turn out and when cool cut the cake into two halves. Sandwich together with whipped cream.

Mushrooms

At this time of year you may still find Parasols, Ceps and Field and Horse Mushrooms. I found an abundance of Clitocybe Geotropes (Clitocybe Geotropa) at this time of year which are edible and a very good size. Do not confuse with Clitocybe Rivulosa which is poisonous (best to refer to a good field guide or ask an expert). Sliced up the Geotropes are delicious pan fried in butter and topped with a little parsley and lemon juice. Whatever wild mushrooms you find, there are various delicious things you can do with them from making a soup, a risotto or a croustade to putting them in a casserole or an omelette.

SOME GENERAL WILD MUSHROOM RECIPES
FOR YOUR AUTUMNAL FINDS

OVEN-BAKED WILD MUSHROOM RISOTTO
Serves 2 – 3

2 tbsp olive oil
1 onion, peeled and sliced
100g, 4oz unsmoked back bacon, chopped
225g, 8oz any wild mushrooms
175g, 6oz risotto rice
600ml, 1pt Marigold Swiss vegetable bouillon stock
75g, 3oz mature Cheddar cheese, grated
a knob of butter
1 tbsp fresh parsley, chopped

Heat the oil in a large frying pan and add the onion and bacon.
Fry until crispy, add the mushrooms and fry for a couple more
minutes. Add the rice and stir to coat in oil. Pour on the stock
and bring to the boil. Transfer to an ovenproof dish and bake
in the oven at gas mark 3, 160°C (325°F) for 20 minutes. Stir
in the cheese and cook for another 10 minutes. Add the butter
and stir it through the risotto. Sprinkle with parsley and serve.

PORK AND MUSHROOM CASSEROLE
Serves 3 – 4

2 tbsp sunflower oil
450g, 1lb diced pork shoulder
1 onion, peeled and sliced
1 carrot, peeled and sliced
1 tbsp plain flour
300ml, ½pt Marigold Swiss vegetable bouillon stock

300ml, ½pt cider
2 bay leaves
225g, 8oz wild mushrooms, such as ceps, oyster mushrooms,
blewits or any others you find
salt and pepper

Heat the oil in a casserole and fry the pieces of pork first to seal; then add the onion and carrot and fry for another couple of minutes. Sprinkle on the flour and then pour on the stock and cider. Add the bay leaves, mushrooms, salt and pepper. Cover and cook in the oven at gas mark 3,160°C (325°F) for a couple of hours, stirring every so often and adding a little water if the casserole becomes too dry.

WILD MUSHROOM TAGLIATELLE
Serves 4

225g, 8oz wild mushrooms
2 tbsp olive oil
1 clove of garlic, peeled and crushed
175g, 6oz unsmoked streaky bacon, grilled and chopped
150ml, ¼pt crème fraîche
1 tsp paprika
250g, 9oz tagliatelle
75g, 3oz Parmesan cheese, grated

Fry the mushrooms in the oil, adding the garlic when the mushrooms are nearly cooked. Add the bacon and crème fraîche and stir, sprinkling in the paprika. Cook the pasta until al dente. Toss the tagliatelle in with the mushroom and bacon mixture and serve with the Parmesan cheese.

WILD MUSHROOM PATÉ
Serves 4 - 6

50g, 2oz dried cranberries
2 tbsp Madeira
25g, 1oz butter
2 shallots, peeled and sliced
1 garlic clove, peeled and crushed
225g, 8oz mixed wild mushrooms
1 sprig of thyme
100g, 4oz cream cheese
1 tbsp balsamic vinegar

Soak the cranberries in the Madeira and leave for a couple of hours. Melt the butter in a frying pan and sauté the onion, garlic and mushrooms in the butter. Put in a processor and whiz with the thyme, cream cheese and balsamic vinegar. Stir in the cranberries and Madeira.

LATE AUTUMN
November

This is a good month for root crops. You will be able to harvest parsnips, swede, celeriac, Jerusalem artichokes, salsify and scorzonera. Medlars are one of the only fruits in season this month. In the wild there are still some greens you can pick such as yarrow and chickweed. There are also some roots you can dig up – roots from silverweed, cat's tail, star of Bethlehem, white waterlily and evening primrose are all edible. Mushrooms should still be around – honey fungus, saffron milk caps, blewits and oyster mushrooms feature in this section.

CULTIVATED VEGETABLES

PARSNIPS - Pastinaca sativa

Parsnips have been cultivated around the Eastern Mediterranean since ancient times. Certainly the Greeks and Romans used parsnips – Pliny refers to pastinaca, probably meaning carrots and parsnips, in the 1st century AD. Parsnips were sent to Emperor Tiberius in Rome every year from Germany where they grew in profusion along the Rhine Valley. It is possible that the Celts in that part of Europe had brought the parsnip back from their travels to the East hundreds of years before. In the Middle Ages the roots were used for medicinal purposes for treating toothache, swollen testicles and stomach aches. There is evidence that parsnips were used as animal fodder in Europe in the 16th century and today Italy still feeds parsnips to the pigs bred for best quality Parma ham. Parsnips have long been used as a sweetener (sugar beet was not developed until the 19th century) and indeed parsnips have a higher sugar content than sugar beet.

The parsnip is a hardy biennial. Seeds sown in March will produce parsnips ready for harvesting in November so they will occupy your patch for a long time. It is said that after a frost a parsnip's flavour will improve. Recommended varieties are Avonresister (which is resistant to canker) Tender and True, Gladiator and White Gem. Parsnips contain some Vitamin C, B1, and beta-carotene and are a reasonable source of iron.

CURRIED PARSNIP AND APPLE SOUP
Serves 4 - 6

25g, 1oz butter
1 tbsp oil
1 tbsp curry powder
450g, 1lb parsnips, sliced
225g, 8oz cooking apples, peeled and chopped
225g, 8oz onions, chopped
600ml, 1pt chicken stock
150ml, ¼pt milk
150ml, ¼pt white wine
salt and pepper
2 crisp eating apples, cored and chopped

Melt the butter and oil in a heavy saucepan and add the chopped onions. Then stir in the curry powder, parsnips and cooking apples. Cook together gently for 10 minutes. Add the stock, milk and wine, bring to the boil and simmer for 30 minutes or until the parsnips are soft. Purée in a food processor or blender. Reheat and if liked add the two chopped eating apples just before serving.

PARSNIP CAKE
Serves 6 – 8

150g, 5oz self raising flour
2 tsp baking powder
1 tsp ground cinnamon
100g, 4oz brown sugar
3 eggs
180ml, 6fl oz rapeseed oil (or sunflower oil)
100g, 4oz parsnips, peeled and grated
75g, 3oz pecans, chopped

Cream cheese topping
100g, 4oz cream cheese
50g, 2oz butter
150g, 5oz icing sugar

Sieve together the flour, baking powder and cinnamon. Mix in the brown sugar. Make a well in the centre and gradually beat in the eggs, oil, parsnip and pecans. Spoon into a greased 20cm, 8in cake tin and bake in the oven at gas mark 4, 180°C (350°F) for 30 minutes. Turn the cake out. For the topping beat together the cream cheese, butter and icing sugar and spread over the cake.

SWEDE - Brassica napus

The swede originated, not surprisingly, in Sweden arriving in Britain around 1781. A hybrid between a turnip and a cabbage, in times of famine the swede was a useful food for poorer people. Cooked swede is good mashed or puréed with potato or added to casseroles and stews. Seeds need to be sown in early June. You should be able to harvest them from October but swedes are hardy so can be left in the soil until December or January when other vegetables are scarce. Swedes supply some vitamin C and are a source of niacin (vitamin B).

SWEDE AND APPLE PURÉE
Serves 6

This is a simple vegetable dish which goes well with pork or chicken.

900g, 2lb swedes, peeled and sliced
50g, 2oz butter
350g, 12oz cooking apples, peeled, cored and sliced
salt and pepper
a pinch of nutmeg
1 tsp caster sugar
1 tbsp double cream

Boil the swedes until soft and then mash with the butter until smooth. Cook the apples in a little water until tender and stir into the swede purée. Add salt, pepper, nutmeg and sugar. A spoonful of double cream may also be added.

SWEDE WITH BACON
Serves 4

1 swede, peeled and cut into cubes
15g, ½oz butter
4 rashers streaky unsmoked bacon
pinch of pepper
pinch of nutmeg
2 tbsp single cream

Cook the swede in boiling salted water for about 20 minutes or until tender. Drain and mash it with the butter. Dry fry the bacon until crisp and chop into small pieces. Stir the bacon into the swede purée with some pepper and nutmeg. Lastly stir in the cream.

JERUSALEM ARTICHOKES - Helianthus tuberosus

Jerusalem artichokes will be ready for digging up in November and you can keep digging them up through December and January. In February they will start sprouting again for a new season's growth. Jerusalem artichokes have nothing to do with Jerusalem nor with globe artichokes but it is thought that the word is a corruption of the Italian word 'Girasole', meaning sunflower and literally 'turning in the sun'. They are related to sunflowers and grow in a similar way. These root tubers originated in North America, or more exactly in Nova Scotia, where the French found them in the 17th century. The French brought them back to Europe and the Dutch grew them extensively before exporting them to Britain. Artichokes have a nutty taste but are not popular with everyone due to their ability to produce wind when eaten. As a result of their effect on the digestive system they are nicknamed 'fartichokes'. They are also very knobbly and difficult to peel which may put some people off growing them but they're a useful vegetable to have in the winter and work particularly well in soups.

Artichokes are incredibly easy to grow and rather like mint they spread, growing back every year because there will always be tubers left in the ground. Like sunflowers, Jerusalem artichokes grow very tall, to about 3m, 10ft but their leaves are smaller and they only actually flower in very hot summers. Tubers can be purchased from seed suppliers/ garden centres or from tubers saved from the year before. Artichokes will grow in almost any soil but well-manured clay soils produce the heaviest crops. Once the plants have reached their full height their stalks may easily be blown over in the wind but you can cut the stalks back in the autumn without damaging the tubers; dig up the tubers whenever you require them through the winter. Artichokes contain inulin which promotes good bacteria and detoxes the colon - they are low in calories and have moderate amounts of Vitamins B1 and 5.

ARTICHOKE SOUP
Serves 4

1 medium onion, peeled and sliced
3 tbsp olive oil
1 medium potato, peeled and sliced
675g, 1½lb Jerusalem artichokes, peeled and sliced
900ml, 1½pt Marigold Swiss vegetable bouillon stock
1 tsp fresh thyme, chopped
2 tbsp crème fraîche
1 tbsp chopped parsley

Sauté the onion in the olive oil in a large saucepan and add the sliced potato. Add the artichokes and allow to cook for several minutes. After a couple of minutes pour in the stock. Bring to the boil and then cover and allow to simmer for 30 minutes, stirring every so often. Purée the mixture in a liquidizer or food processor and reheat if necessary before serving. Add a dollop of crème fraîche and some parsley into each bowl of soup before serving.

ARTICHOKES WITH THICK TOMATO SAUCE
Serves 4 – 6

1 onion, peeled and sliced
1 clove of garlic, peeled and crushed
3 tbsp olive oil
450g, 1lb Jerusalem artichokes, peeled and sliced
1 x 400g, 14oz tin of tomatoes
1 tbsp tomato purée
1 tbsp chopped parsley

Fry the onion and garlic in the olive oil for several minutes in a large frying pan until softened. Add the sliced artichokes and cook for 5 minutes. Add the tin of tomatoes and the purée and cook covered for 25 minutes. Add the parsley and serve. The artichokes should still have a bit of a crunch to them.

CELERIAC - **Apium graveolens**

Celeriac has a flavour like celery and is really just a turnip-rooted form of the same plant. The roots make a good substitute for celery in winter and it is easier to grow but does need a long growing season. Sow the seeds in pots in March and transplant the seedlings outdoors in June. As the plants grow and the roots start swelling, remove any side growths. The roots should be ready for lifting in October but leave them in the ground and use them in November when not much else is available.

CELERIAC REMOULADE
Serves 4 – 6

450g, 1lb celeriac, peeled and cut into strips
2 tbsp Dijon mustard
3 tbsp mayonnaise
1 tsp lemon juice
3 tbsp soured cream
1 tsp chopped parsley
1 tsp chopped chives

Blanch the celeriac in boiling water for 2 minutes. Drain and transfer to a serving bowl. Blend the mustard with the mayonnaise, lemon juice and soured cream. Fold into the celeriac and sprinkle with the parsley and chives.

SALSIFY AND SCORZONERA
Tragopogon porrifolius and **Scorzonera hispanica**

These are similar vegetables and scorzonera is also known as black salsify because it has a black skin. Salisfy is known as vegetable oyster because it has an oyster-like flavour. These vegetables are grown like parsnips for their roots. You can plant seeds in April and although the roots may be ready for digging in October you can leave them until November or dig as required right the way through the winter as the roots are hardy. If you leave them until March they will have produced tender shoots and you can add to salads or cook as a green vegetable.

CULTIVATED FRUITS

MEDLARS - Mespilus germanica

Medlar trees originated in Persia. They were familiar to the Greeks and Romans – Theophrastus mentioned them and later Pliny referred to three different types of medlar. The name, medlar, derives from the Greek for 'mesos' meaning half and 'pilos' meaning ball. They were once popular in Britain reaching their peak during the Middle Ages in Europe. Charlemagne decreed that the medlar be planted on the royal estates and medlars were common in monastery gardens. In Victorian times they were reasonably popular and used to be served at the end of a meal with port. Today medlar trees are a rare sight and the fruit is not widely used or known about. If you are lucky, you might know someone with a medlar tree in his or her garden – the fruit is prolific and you don't need many to make a medlar jelly. Occasionally a tree might be found in a hedgerow in the South of England. You will be highly unlikely to find medlars on sale anywhere. Medlar trees are similar to pear trees, being fairly low with branches, and often the trunk, contorted. The leaves are lance-shaped and the tree produces white, scentless flowers in May. The fruit is greenish-yellow when unripe, looking like a small apple and later on looks like a giant brown rose hip with its five tailed calyx sticking out from the head of the fruit like a crown. The French have a rather rude term for them – 'cul de chien'!

Medlar fruits have to be half rotten or 'bletted' before they are edible. This is obviously not such a good climate as the Mediterranean as the fruits here do not have time to fully ripen on the tree. They should be picked in November or left to fall and stored until they become soft and look like a rotten pear. The foliage turns a beautiful reddish brown in the autumn. The fruit, once bletted, can be eat with a little cream and sugar but first you have to extract the flesh from the five large pips and discard the skin which can prove arduous. The taste is difficult to describe – it is a bit like apple purée with a hint of cinnamon. Some say they taste like dates. Nutritionally medlars are high in potassium.

MEDLAR JELLY
Makes just over 1kg, 2½lb

1.8kg, 4lb medlars, bletted or half bletted and half unripe
water to cover
juice of 1 lemon
granulated sugar

Wash the medlars and put into a large saucepan with water to cover. Add the lemon juice and bring to the boil. Simmer for about 1 hour by which time the fruit will be very soft. Strain the fruit through muslin without squeezing. Measure the liquid and for every 600ml or 1pt of juice use 450g or 1lb of sugar. Heat the juice gently with the sugar in a large preserving pan until the sugar has dissolved. Bring to the boil and test for a set after about 15 minutes. When ready pour into warmed jars and seal.

MEDLAR PURÉE WITH CREAM AND SUGAR

450g, 1lb medlars
75g, 3oz brown sugar
150ml, ¼pt thick cream
½ tsp ground cinnamon

Sieve the medlars and mix the purée with brown sugar, cream and cinnamon.

IN THE WILD
Roots

SILVERWEED ROOTS (silverweed = Potentilla anserine)

Silverweed is widespread in damp grassy and waste places and has toothed fern-like silvery leaves and yellow flowers. The roots are small but taste like parsnips. Dig the roots up in late autumn, wash them and scrape away the outer skin. They used to be much enjoyed in the Hebrides when other food was scarce. The roots can be boiled or baked as with other root vegetables. These roots were actually cultivated in Britain as a useful vegetable right up until the introduction of the potato.

CAT'S TAIL
Also known as Reedmace or Bulrush - Typha latifolia

Not to be confused with the true bulrush, this plant is a tall perennial with long, sword-like, flat leaves. The stout stem which can be up to 2m, 7ft tall is topped by the 'mace', a brown tube shaped spike of female flowers with an upper narrow spear of yellow male flowers. After flowering between June and

August, seeds develop surrounded by brown cottony hairs. Cat's tail is common throughout Britain beside ponds, lakes and reedy swamps. It likes wet soil and lots of sun. All parts of the plant are edible. The roots can be grated and eaten raw, boiled and eaten like potatoes or dried and ground into powder. Young shoots can be gathered in the spring and used like asparagus but you should peel the outer skin – they taste like cucumber. They are also known as Cossack Asparagus. The flowering spike can be eaten raw or cooked and tastes like sweet corn. The seeds have a nutty taste.

STAR OF BETHLEHEM - Ornithogalum umbellatum

This plant is so called because it has white star-shaped flowers and is prevalent in Palestine. Star of Bethlehem is poisonous to cattle but we can eat the bulbous root. Peel the bulbs and eat as a boiled vegetable or eat raw. In the East the bulbs are roasted like chestnuts. They used to be dried and sold in the streets of Cairo and Damascus to people going on long journeys across the desert.

WHITE WATERLILY - **Nymphaea alba**

The underwater tubers of the white waterlily are edible when boiled as a vegetable.

EVENING PRIMROSE - **Oenothera biennis**

This biennial plant has yellow trumpet-shaped flowers. It is not a true wild plant but is supposedly an escapee from gardens. It flowers from June. Evening primrose is valued for its root which has a flavour like parsnips and should be used like salsify.

Mushrooms

HONEY FUNGUS - **Armillaria mellea**

Honey fungi are usually found late in the autumn growing in clusters round the base of deciduous or coniferous trees. These fungi are a dangerous parasite of trees and ultimately cause the trees they infect to die. The fungus spreads by long black cords called rhizomorphs which look like bootlaces and are found under the bark, on roots or in the soil. The mushrooms are orange coloured and are best cooked before eaten but use only the caps as the stalks are very tough. Honey fungus is rich in flavour and good added to casseroles.

SAFFRON MILK CAPS - Lactarius deliciosus

Saffron milk caps grow under pine trees in late autumn. They are orange with short stems and the caps have bands of deep orange with a depression in the centre. The gills are also orange and produce orange milk. When bruised the cap will gradually turn green. Milk caps give off a lot of liquid during cooking so fry until it evaporates. Try serving these on toast.

BLEWITS Also known as blue legs - Tricholoma

Field and wood blewits can be found at this time of year, named after the bluish-violet tinge on their stems. Field blewits grow in fields in the late autumn in large rings and they can be difficult to spot because their flat irregular caps can look like dead leaves scattered over a field. Blewits are tender and somewhat watery when cooked. Fry in butter and add to a bechamel sauce.

OYSTER MUSHROOMS - Pleurotus ostreatus

Oyster mushrooms are bracket fungi growing on logs, tree trunks or branches especially on beeches and poplars. They grow in clusters in tiers and can be up to 20cm, 8in across. The caps look like shells with uncurled edges and are grey or slate-blue in colour and the flesh white, soft and rubbery. Pick them when young and use in soups, risottos and to make fritters. Mix them with other mushrooms and try the recipes over the page.

MUSHROOM GOUGÈRE
Serves 4

For the Choux Pastry
150ml, ¼pt water + 50g, 2oz butter
65g, 2½oz plain flour, sifted onto a plate
2 eggs, beaten
50g, 2oz Cheddar cheese, grated

Filling
15g, ½oz butter
1 onion
1 tbsp plain flour
150ml, ¼pt Marigold Swiss vegetable bouillon stock
150ml, ¼pt milk
175g, 6oz mixed wild mushrooms
6 cherry tomatoes, halved
1 tbsp Cheddar cheese, grated
1 tbsp breadcrumbs
½ tsp thyme, fresh or dried

To make the choux pastry, place the water and butter in a saucepan and bring to the boil. Turn off the heat and quickly beat in all the flour. Beat until the mixture forms a ball. Beat in the eggs, a little at a time and when the mixture is smooth and glossy stir in the cheese. Spoon the mixture around the sides of a greased 20cm, 8in flan dish. For the filling melt the butter in a saucepan, add the onion and fry until softened, adding the mushrooms after a couple of minutes. Stir in the flour and then gradually stir in the stock and milk and cook until thickened. Add the tomatoes and spoon into the choux pastry ring. Scatter the cheese, breadcrumbs and thyme over the top. Cook in the oven at gas mark 5, 190°C (375°F) for 30 minutes.

WILD MUSHROOM RISOTTO
Serves 3 – 4

3 tbsp olive oil
225g, 8oz mixed wild mushrooms
225g, 8oz risotto rice
1 tsp tomato purée
120ml, 4fl oz white wine
600ml, 1pt Marigold Swiss vegetable bouillon stock
50g, 2oz butter
50g, 2oz mature Cheddar cheese, grated

Fry the mushrooms in some of the oil until quite crispy. Set aside. Heat the rest of the oil and sauté the onions. Add the rice and tomato purée and then gradually add the wine and stock, stirring until absorbed before you add more stock. When all the liquid has been absorbed, stir in the mushrooms and add the butter and cheese. Stir through allowing the butter and cheese to melt before serving.

EARLY WINTER
December

In the winter on a mild day you can start your vegetables off by planting broad beans, onion sets, lettuces preferably under cloches and garlic. Leeks are at their best for picking this month as are Brussels sprouts, radicchio and endives. You can still pick kale and Jerusalem artichokes. Winter purslane is a very useful salad ingredient at this time of year (see page 214) and there are various oriental salad leaves that will survive the winter such as mizuna, red giant mustard and green-in-snow mustard leaves; also mustard golden streaks and mustard red frills are attractive and very tasty and mine survived through the winter. Rocket leaves should also be fine and Swiss chard will continue to produce leaves. In the wild it is still possible to pick haws and Alexanders but goose grass, shepherd's purse, chickweed, wintercress and yarrow are all at their best and feature under this month. On the fungi front you can search for Jew's ears and velvet shanks, and on the seashore you can still find sea beet.

CULTIVATED VEGETABLES

LEEKS - Allium ampeloprasum

Grow some leeks which you can harvest in December when very little else is available. Musselburgh is an old established variety which is very winter hardy and will be ready for cropping from December onwards.

Leeks were cultivated by the Egyptians. The Greeks ate them and Hippocrates believed that leeks were a cure for nose bleeds. The Romans were keen growers of leeks; Nero in particular was enthusiastic about eating them saying they helped clear his voice. Roman legions brought the leek to Wales and it soon became the National Emblem. To celebrate a famous battle victory in which King Cadwallader beat the Saxons in AD640, Welsh soldiers wore leeks in their hats. As a result March 1st is celebrated as St David's Day and the Welsh still wear leeks in their hats. There is a saying, 'Eat leeks in March and wild garlic in May and all year after physicians may play'. Leeks are easy to grow as they are very hardy but they need a long season to mature. Sow seeds in the middle of March and then in July transfer the seedlings to their final position.

When preparing leeks for cooking, be really careful to remove all the dirt which is often hidden behind the outer leaves. The Scots were great lovers of leeks and invented the famous soup: cock-a-leekie. Not everyone likes leeks and my children have never really enjoyed them but they are a useful winter vegetable. Leeks are rich in potassium and iron and contain Vitamins B and C.

LEEK PURÉE WITH BUTTER AND
A TOUCH OF CREAM
Serves 4 - 6

1kg, 2.2lb leeks, washed
50g, 2oz butter
2 tbsp double cream
salt and pepper

Slice the leeks but only use the white part. The green part tends to be too strong when only lightly cooked. Fry in half the butter for 5 minutes. Then purée in the food processor with the rest of the butter and double cream. Add salt and pepper to taste.

BRUSSELS SPROUTS - Brassica oleracea

Brussels sprouts were first developed in Brussels in Belgium in the 1200s but it was not until the late 1800s that sprouts were grown here. Britain is now the most important and climatically acceptable centre of production in the world. The plant is extremely hardy, enduring the coldest conditions and so ideal for the variable British winter. Sprouts need a long season of growth and unless you use manure and make sure the soil is very firm you may not get a good crop. In this case they are probably not worth growing as you will get only a few sprouts on each plant and they do take up a lot of space.

You can sow seeds in a cold frame in January and then plant them out in May or June. Otherwise you can pick up seedlings at garden centres and plant them out in late spring. They begin to crop in October and continue until March, spanning the coldest months of the year, and therefore providing you with veg when other greens are scarce. Individual sprouts develop on the stems from the bottom upwards. As you pick the sprouts strip the corresponding leaves from the stem. If the leaves turn yellow you must pick the sprouts and get rid of any yellow leaves at the same time. A good plant will produce sprouts very close together. Taller plants may need to be staked. To pick the sprouts snap the buttons off with a downward pressure of the thumb. The plants will develop a canopy of leaves at the top which resemble mini cabbages and can be picked and cooked as for cabbages when you have picked all the sprouts. However if early sprouts are cut instead of picked you may be lucky and get a second crop that you can harvest after Christmas. There are now various F1 Hybrids that you can buy as seeds which produce a heavy crop over a longer period.

Brussels are high in fibre, folate and vitamin C. They also contain phytochemicals which fight against cancer.

BRUSSEL SPROUTS WITH
HAZELNUTS AND BACON
Serves 6

1kg, 2.2lb Brussels sprouts
225g, 8oz unsmoked back bacon, chopped
25g, 1oz butter
50g, 2oz hazelnuts

Steam the sprouts for 5 minutes. Melt the butter in a frying pan and fry the bacon and nuts until lightly browned. Add the sprouts and toss to combine. Cook gently for another 3 minutes. Serve at once.

SPROUTS AND CARROTS IN
TOMATO CREAM SAUCE
Serves 2 - 3

225g, 8oz Brussels sprouts
1 large carrot, peeled and sliced
15g, ½oz butter
15g, ½oz plain flour
150ml, ¼pt Marigold Swiss vegetable bouillon stock
120ml, 4fl oz milk
1 tbsp tomato purée
25g, 1oz mature Cheddar cheese, grated

Steam the sprouts and carrots together for 5 minutes. Make the sauce as you would a Bechamel sauce by melting the butter, stirring in the flour and then gradually adding the stock, tomato purée and milk. Transfer the veg to a small ovenproof dish and sprinkle the cheese on top. Finish off under a hot grill and serve at once.

RADICCHIO AND ENDIVE - Cichorium intybus

It is thought that endive was eaten by the Egyptians. It was well known to the Romans and is mentioned by Ovid, Horace and Pliny. It wasn't introduced to Europe until the 1500s and we know it was grown in English gardens at that time.

Radicchio and endive are part of the chicory family. There are three types of chicory – red chicory or radicchio has been introduced comparatively recently from Italy. The lower temperatures in the autumn and winter make their leaves turn a beautiful crimson although there are now some varieties which are naturally red and heart earlier. Radicchio, like broccoli, contains the phytochemical sulforophane.

There are two types of endive – Batavian or escarole is an upright plant with large leaves. Then there is curly endive with serrated leaves which can be harvested in late summer and added to salads. The leaves are slightly bitter. The Batavian type, which can be blanched, is included here as it is a useful winter salad vegetable. Sow Batavian types in August. Blanch endives in November when the leaves are dry; bind them together with string to make a heart and cover with an upturned flower pot. After three weeks the centres of the plants will have turned a creamy-white shade. Use as soon as possible. There is also a frizzy endive called Wallonne which develops a large head and self-blanching heart and you can harvest in November, December and January.

The third type of chicory used for forcing as chicons is dealt with in the January and February section (see page 15).

ENDIVE, EGG AND ANCHOVY SALAD
Serves 3 – 4

small tin of anchovy fillets
4 hard-boiled eggs, shelled

1 tbsp white wine vinegar
3 tbsp olive oil
1 head of endive

Drain the anchovies of oil and mash up with two of the eggs. Add the vinegar and oil and stir together. Leave to stand for 30 minutes. Tear up the endive leaves and arrange them in a serving bowl. Pour the anchovy sauce over them. Slice the remaining eggs and arrange on top.

RADICCHIO, EGG AND AVOCADO SALAD
Serves 3 - 4

Half a radicchio
3 eggs, hard-boiled, shelled and halved
1 avocado, peeled and sliced
1 tomato, chopped
100g, 4oz sweetcorn
1 tbsp sunflower seeds

Creamy dressing
1 tbsp caster sugar
2 tbsp lemon juice
1 tsp Dijon mustard
pinch of paprika
120ml, 4fl oz crème fraîche

Separate the radicchio leaves and arrange in a serving dish. Slice the eggs and arrange over the leaves along with the avocado and tomato. Scatter sweetcorn and sunflower seeds over the salad. Make the dressing by mixing together the sugar, lemon juice, mustard and paprika with some salt and pepper. Stir in the crème fraîche and chill. Just before serving the salad pour the dressing over it.

CULTIVATED SALAD HERBS

There are various salad herbs that you can grow in your garden that will be available almost all the year round and that are useful at this time of year. **WINTER PURSLANE** is an annual (also known as claytonia or miner's lettuce) – sow a row in late summer under a cloche if possible and it should keep you going in the winter. It produces small white flowers in spring. The succulent leaves, flowers and stalks are all edible (see also Summer Purslane) **SALAD BURNET** is also a useful salad herb which usually survives through a mild winter – the leaves are small and dainty and have a cucumber flavour.

IN THE WILD
Wild Greens

GOOSEGRASS Also known as Cleavers, Sticky Billy, Sticky Willie or Hug Me Close – Galium aparine

Goosegrass is that familiar common plant which sticks to your clothes. The stems and leaves have hooked hairs and the name goosegrass comes from the fact that it used to be a plant fed to goslings. The plant can be picked in winter, particularly in frosty weather when there is little else about. Pick it before the hard round seeds appear and cook like spinach. Alternatively you can add it to soups.

SHEPHERD'S PURSE - Capsella bursa-pastoris

Shepherd's purse is a widespread, self-perpetuating annual that grows in any kind of soil and in any kind of habitat from waste places to arable fields and is distinctive with its rosette of leaves pressed very close to the ground. It is so called because the heart-shaped seed pods look like the type of purse carried by shepherds in the Middle Ages. Shepherd's purse has little white flowers that can, like chickweed, be seen in most months of the year. It contains vitamin C and calcium. The leaves are aromatic and pungent, containing a volatile oil similar to mustard, and taste a bit like cress. Use the leaves like cabbage.

CHICKWEED Also known as Chick Wittles, Chicken's Meat and Mischievous Jack   - Stellaria media

Chickweed is pretty much available most of the year and adds a subtle taste to a mixed salad. This is a very common garden weed which actually grows, flowers and self-seeds all year round. It spreads but is a low growing plant. It may well appear in your vegetable garden. The pale green, small leaves have a mild flavour, quite like cress. The leaves are nutritious containing vitamin C and phosphorus. If you gather enough you can also cook chickweed like spinach. Chickweed is known to be good for itchy skin. Apparently fresh leaves in a poultice relieve inflammation. Chickweed is so named precisely because it is much loved by young birds and chickens.

CHICKWEED SALAD
Serves 2

1 bunch of chickweed
100g, 4oz streaky smoked bacon, grilled and chopped
2 hard boiled eggs, peeled and halved
2 tbsp vinaigrette dressing

Scatter the chickweed over a serving plate, followed by the chopped bacon. Arrange the halved eggs over the top and dress with the vinaigrette.

CHICKWEED SOUP

I actually made ths soup in July and was able to use all the ingredients from the garden, apart from the oil and stock!

2 tbsp olive oil
5 spring onions, sliced
1 potato, peeled and sliced
1 lettuce, shredded
1 large bunch of chickweed
900ml, 1½pts Marigold Swiss vegetable bouillon stock

Heat the oil in a saucepan and fry the spring onions and potato until softened. Add the lettuce and chickweed and stir. Add the stock, bring to the boil and then simmer for 20 minutes. Liquidise the soup, reheat if necessary and serve with a dollop of crème fraîche if liked.

COMMON WINTERCRESS Also known as Yellow Rocket - Barbarea vulgaris

Common wintercress grows throughout Britain but is more common in the South – it is a biennial or perennial and it particularly likes wet places, growing in hedges or on the banks of streams. The leaves are dark green, shiny and oval-shaped. You can use it in a salad but it has a hot flavour. You can also cook it like spinach.

YARROW - Achillea millefolium

This is a perennial common all over Britain on all soils and to be found in grassy areas, hedgerows and roadside verges. It is like a little fern in appearance and used to have a reputation for healing wounds. This dates back to Achilles who used yarrow to staunch his soldiers' wounds, as instructed by wise Chiron the Centaur. In his honour the plant was given its Latin name Achillea millefollium. It flowers from June to October. The whole plant can be gathered. You can also buy yarrow as a potted herb - I have seen it for sale in my local market. You can add yarrow to salads although it is quite bitter. You can also make yarrow tea which is a traditional remedy for helping sweat out a fever. Apparently yarrow opens the pores which in turn instigates sweating.

YARROW TEA

Infuse the two or three stalks of yarrow, including leaves and flowers, in a cup of boiling water for 4 minutes, then strain and serve. You can sweeten with sugar or honey.

YARROW AND BEETROOT SALAD
Serves 2

Bunch of yarrow leaves
1 cooked beetroot, sliced

Soured cream dressing
2 tsp sugar
1 tbsp lemon juice
½ tsp Dijon mustard
pinch of paprika
salt and pepper to taste
4 tbsp soured cream

Chop the yarrow up. Scatter the yarrow over the beetroot in a small salad bowl. For the dressing mix together the sugar, lemon juice, mustard, paprika, salt and pepper. Add the soured cream. Pour over the beetroot and yarrow and serve.

Mushrooms

VELVET SHANKS – Flammulina velutipes

These little orange mushrooms are named after their furry stalks and only grow in mid winter, often starting to grow after a frost. Other mushrooms are killed off by frost but this one survives the coldest temperatures. It can also be completely frozen and then revive as it thaws! The Velvet Shank grows on decaying or dead wood, particularly on elm tree trunks and sometimes on oak in large clusters. Velvet Shanks have a good taste but are a little chewy so work best in a slow cooked dish such as in a casserole or soup.

USEFUL CONTACTS
FRUIT GROWERS AND SUPPLIERS

Brogdale Horticultural Trust, Brogdale Road, Faversham ME13 8XZ
Tel: 01795 535286 www.brogdale.org.uk

Deacon's Nursery, Moor View, Godshill, Isle of Wight PO38 3HW
Tel: 01983 840750 www.deaconsnurseryfruits.co.uk

Ken Muir Ltd, Honeypot Farm, Rectory Road, Weeley Heath,
Clacton-on-Sea CO16 9BJ Tel: 01255 8301811 www.kenmuir.co.uk

Keepers Nursery, Gallants Court, East Farleigh, Maidstone ME15
0LE Tel: 01622 726465 www.keepers-nursery.co.uk

VEGETABLE AND HERB SEED SUPPLIERS

Suffolk Herbs, Monks Farm, Coggeshall Road, Kelvedon CO5 9PG
Tel: 01376 572456 www.suffolkherbs.com

Edwin Tucker & Sons, Brewery Meadow, Stonepark, Ashburton
TQ13 7DG Tel: 01364 652233 www.edwintucker.com

Seeds of Italy, Phoenix Industrial Estate, Rosslyn Crescent, Harrow
HA1 2SP Tel: 020 8427 5020 www.seedsofitaly.com

Organic Gardening Catalogue, Riverdene, Molesey Road, Hersham
KT12 4RG Tel: 0845 1301304 www.OrganicCatalogue.com

Jekka's Herb Farm, Rose Cottage, Shellards Lane, Alveston, Bristol BS35 3SY Tel: 01454 418878 www.jekkasherbfarm.com

FRUIT AND VEGETABLE SEED SUPPLIERS

D T Brown, Bury Road, Newmarket CB8 7PQ Tel: 0845 1662275
www.dtbrownseeds.co.uk

Index